INDIAN RECIPES

Delicious & Easy Indian Recipes You Can Make Fast With Simple Ingredients

(The Ultimate Electric Pressure Cooker Cookbook for Cooking)

Angela Bartz

Published by Alex Howard

© **Angela Bartz**

All Rights Reserved

Indian Recipes: Delicious & Easy Indian Recipes You Can Make Fast With Simple Ingredients (The Ultimate Electric Pressure Cooker Cookbook for Cooking)

ISBN 978-1-77485-023-7

All rights reserved. No part of this guide may be reproduced in any form without permission in writing from the publisher except in the case of brief quotations embodied in critical articles or reviews.

Legal & Disclaimer

The information contained in this book is not designed to replace or take the place of any form of medicine or professional medical advice. The information in this book has been provided for educational and entertainment purposes only.

The information contained in this book has been compiled from sources deemed reliable, and it is accurate to the best of the Author's knowledge; however, the Author cannot guarantee its accuracy and validity and cannot be held liable for any errors or omissions. Changes are periodically made to this book. You must consult your doctor or get professional medical advice before using any of the suggested remedies, techniques, or information in this book.

Table of contents

Part 1 1

Indian Recipes 2

Anda Burjie (Spicy Indian Scrambled Eggs) 2

Sooji Upma (Indian Semolina Breakfast Dish) 5

Masala Dosa (Sourdough Crepes) 8

Spelt Appams – Yeast Pancakes 12

Spicy Scones with Tomato Chutney Recipe 15

Baked Beet Samosas 18

Ingredients: 18

Kedgeree 21

Ingredients: 22

Chicken Biryani 24

Haleem 28

Sprouted Mung Chaat 31

Quick Indian Butter Chicken 34

Vegan Palak Paneer (Tofu in a Mild Spinach Gravy) 37

Kerala Coconut Pork Curr 40

y 40

Time: 1 hour 15 minutes Yield: 6 servings 40

Directions: 42

Tandoori Turkey 43

Halva 45

Ingredients: 45

Date Kheer (Indian Rice Pudding) 47

Gulab Jamun 50

Kulfi 53

Strawberry Lassi with Cherry Liqueur 56

Ingredients: 56

Directions: 57

Chai Tea 58

Roasted Eggplant and Garlic Hummus 60

Part 2 62

Green Onion Bhurji 63

Mysore Bonda 64

Dahi Wada 64

Rasmalai 66

Instant Dhokla 67

Matar Palak 68

Aloo Mutter 69

Venn Pongal 69

Tamilian Kurma 70

Vegetable Korma 71

Mixed Vegetable Kofta in Tomato Curry 72

Chakali 73

Moong Soup With Paneer	74
Healthy Tomato soup	75
Corn Soup with Vegetables	76
Green Peas Skin Soup	77
Hara Nariel Ka Shorba	78
Lentil and Vegetable Broth	79
Letil Soup	80
Tum Yum Soup	81
Sweet Corn Soup	81
RAJMA CURRY	82
MALAI KOFTA CURRY	85
Cheesy Sweet Jamuns	87
Kofta Lajawab	88
Beetroot Parathas	89
Badshahi Baigan	90
Red Tomato Gravy	91
Green Gravy	92
White Gravy	93
Brown Gravy	94
Besan Burfi	97
Raabdi	97
Ras Malai	98
Rasagulla	99

Dum Arvi 100

Dum Aloo 101

Matar Paneer 102

Bhindi Masala 103

Vegetable Jalfrasie 105

Rasam Masala 106

Mangalore Rasam 108

Sambar 110

Cauliflower Curry 111

Sambar Masala 112

Vada 113

Didir Onion Rava Dosa 114

Didir Dosa 115

Dosai 115

Basic Curry Sauce 116

Biryani 117

Double Ka Meetha (Bread Pudding) 119

Indian Cream of Tomato Soup 120

Kadhi 121

Bengan ka bhurta 122

Halwa 123

Toll House Pan Cookie 123

Rasavangi 124

Stuffed Brinjal Curry 125

Maida Bonda 125

Rava Bonda 126

Palak Paneer 126

Coconut Milk Pulav 127

Tomato pickle 127

Lime pickle 128

Ginger Pickle 128

Tamarind pickle (Pulikkachal) 128

Aavakkai (Mango pickle) 129

Gonkura Thokku 129

Curd Vadai 130

Cabbage Vadai 130

Urud Vadai (Medhu vadai) 131

Mutton Rogan Josh 131

Indian Aloo Gobi 134

Paratha with Minced Meat 137

Traditional Palak Paneer 139

Chole Bhature 142

Curried Spicy Egg 145

Chaat Papdi 148

Pav Bhaji Masala 150

Traditional Lamb Vindaloo 153

Traditional Mataba 155

Curry Malai Kofta 158

Indian Aloo Palak 170

Bhindi Masala Fry 172

Chana Pulao 174

Banana Chips 177

Baingan Barta 179

Dum Aloo 181

Indian Fish Fry 183

Aloo Tiki 185

Part 1

Indian Recipes

Anda Burjie (Spicy Indian Scrambled Eggs)

Time: 30 minutes
Yield: 2 servings

Scrambled eggs are a classic breakfast that even beginner cooks can make. This doesn't change with scrambled eggs made Indian style.

Ingredients:

2 tablespoons sunflower seed oil
1 medium red onion, finely chopped
1 medium red bell pepper

1 green chili pepper, split lengthwise
2 teaspoons ginger, minced
1 teaspoon red paprika
1/2 teaspoon turmeric powder
4 eggs
1 tablespoon skim milk
Salt
2 teaspoons butter, room temperature
1/4 cup chopped fresh cilantro, divided

Directions:

1. Whisk the eggs and milk until frothy.
2. Heat oil in a fry pan and swirl the oil around the pan until the base is well coated.
3. Add chopped red onions and sauté for 2 minutes until soft and translucent. Add green chilies, chopped red bell peppers and ginger and stir until fragrant or about half a minute.
4. Reduce heat to low, add red paprika and ground turmeric and lightly mix.
5. Immediately add the whisked eggs and salt and gently stir around with a wooden spoon till the mixture starts to thicken.
6. Increase the heat to high and vigorously stir the egg mixture around to scramble the eggs. Break any large clumps.
7. Stir in half the chopped cilantro and cook until it wilts.

8. Turn the heat off and add a generous dollop of butter on top. Garnish with chopped cilantro. Serve immediately with lightly toasted white bread or flat bread.

Sooji Upma (Indian Semolina Breakfast Dish)

Time: 30 minutes
Yield: 2 servings

Sooji Upma is a dish made out of semolina, which is a flour that has many purposes. One purpose is to cook the flour into a mixture that you'll find different, yet appealing.

Ingredients:
1 cup fine semolina flour
1 1/2 tablespoons butter, softened
1 teaspoon whole black mustard seeds
1 tablespoon whole peanuts (unsalted)

1 small onion chopped (about 1/2 cup)
2 small dried whole red chili peppers, split and deseeded
2 bay leaves
1/2 cup mixed vegetables
1 teaspoon red chili powder
1 teaspoon sugar
1 ripe tomato, chopped
Table salt
2 1/2 cups water

Directions:

1. Place semolina in cast iron pan and roast slowly over medium heat until toasted but not browned, about 3-4 minutes. Transfer to a bowl to cool.

2. Return pan to medium-high, add butter and heat. Add the mustard seeds and let them crackle for about 30 seconds. Add the onion and sauté on medium heat until translucent. Add the whole red chillies, bay leaves and peanuts and stir for 30 seconds until fragrant and the peanuts are lightly browned.

3. Add the mixed vegetables and tomato, cook for 2-3 minutes.

4. Add lightly roasted semolina and stir well to combine with the vegetables to get a coarse, sandy texture.

5. Bring water to a boil in a separate saucepan.

6. Carefully pour the hot water into the semolina in a slow stream, stirring continuously. (Protect your hands as the semolina tends to bubble).

7. Add salt, sugar and paprika powder, mix well. Reduce heat to low and cook for 2 -3 minutes. Stir often to prevent burning at the base, adding hot water little at a time if the mixture dries too quickly. The mixture should be slightly runny at this point.

8. Turn off the heat and keep covered for 2 minutes (the semolina cooks further in the remaining heat). Remove bay leaves. Serve immediately.

Masala Dosa (Sourdough Crepes)

Time: 25 minutes plus 8 hours to ferment
Yield: 4 servings

Dosas can be considered the crepes of the Indian world. With a typically spicy and savory taste, there's no doubt that this is one breakfast that you'll remember.

Ingredients:

For the Masala Dosa:

2 cups medium-grain rice
2 handfuls plain rice krispies (unsweetened)
1/4 pound split black gram
1 teaspoon fenugreek seeds
1/4 cup vegetable oil
2 teaspoons
Cold water as needed

For the Filling:

2 Yukon gold potatoes
1/4 pound onion thinly sliced
2 green chilies split lengthwise
1/4 teaspoon turmeric
6- 8 curry leaves
Salt to taste
1/2 teaspoon mustard seeds
2 tablespoons vegetable oil
1/4 cups hot water
Fresh grated coconut (optional)

Directions:

1. Wash the split black gram and rice and soak in water for 6-8 hours with the fenugreek seeds. Grind to a smooth,

slightly gritty paste about the consistency of pancake batter. Cover and keep aside for 8 to 10 hours in a warm place (about 90° F).

2. Parboil the potatoes in salted water for 8 to 10 minutes. Drain, cool and peel. Cut into 1/2 inch cubes and set aside.

3. In a small skillet, heat oil over medium-high heat. Add the mustard seeds and let them crackle for about 20 seconds. Add the green chilies, sauté until the chilies turn white, add turmeric and give a quick stir to mix. Quickly add onion and sauté until translucent. Add the potatoes and salt. Add the hot water and stir well. Mash the potatoes slightly to release starch.

4. Heat a non-stick frying pan over medium –low heat. Add about 1/2 a teaspoon of oil and swirl it around to coat the pan. Ladle about ¼ cup of the batter into the center of the hot griddle and spread out the batter from center outwards in expanding circles with the back of the ladle (without lifting the ladle from the pan) to get a thin dosa. Drizzle 1/4 teaspoon oil on the edges of the dosa. Cook for 2 -3 minutes until the dosa sets, is golden brown on the underside, and the edges lift from the pan. Loosen with a spatula and lift.

5. Repeat for the remaining dosas, oiling the griddle before each dosa. (Batter keeps for 2 days when refrigerated).

6. Serve hot with a generous helping of the filling at the center, Sprinkle with a teaspoon of grated fresh coconut.

Spelt Appams – Yeast Pancakes

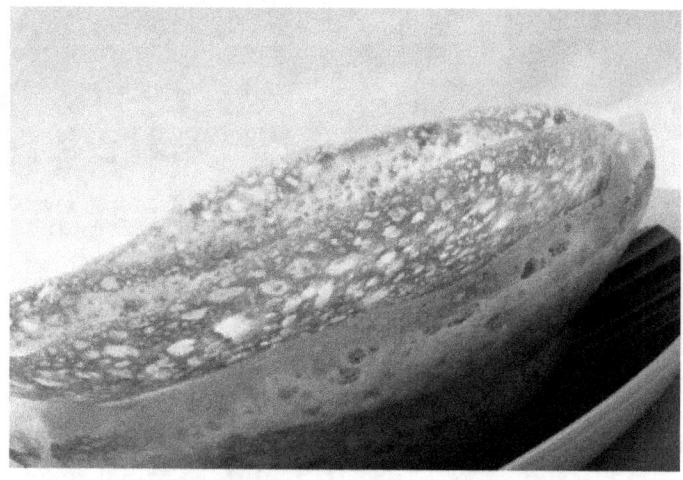

Time: 1 hour, plus 6 hours to ferment
Yield: 8 servings

Here's another Indian spin on a dish we typically eat for breakfast. These Spelt Appams won't be as sweet as a typical pancake, but they have a great taste to compensate.

Ingredients:

1 teaspoon fast action dry yeast
1 cup spelt flour
1/2 cup polenta

1/2 cup coconut cream
4 teaspoons granulated white sugar
1/2 cup fresh thick coconut milk or canned unsweetened coconut milk
Salt to taste
A pinch of ground cardamom (optional)
1-1 1/2 cups lukewarm water (98°F)

Directions:

1. Toast spelt flour in a deep pan over medium heat for about 5-7 minutes until it turns a shade darker. Don't let it brown and stir often. Allow to cool to room temperature.

2. Put 1/2 cup water in a saucepan and stir in the polenta. Heat on medium – low until the mixture starts to boil. Simmer over low heat for 3 minutes until the mixture thickens to porridge like consistency. Then remove from heat and cool to room temperature while stirring often.

3. In a large mixing bowl, combine the spelt flour, fast action yeast, sugar, cooked polenta and 1 cup of lukewarm water, mixing to get a smooth, thick batter, about the consistency of cake batter. Add water a little at a time if necessary if the batter is too thick.

4.   Cover with a plastic film, place in a warm place for 5-6 hours until the batter increases to nearly double the original volume (the batter keeps for up to a day under refrigeration).

5.   Fold in the coconut milk, coconut cream and salt and a pinch of ground cardamom for flavor into the fermented batter.

6.   Heat a large non-stick skillet with a rounded (concave) base over medium- high heat. Brush lightly with oil, ladle out about 1/4 cup of the appam batter into the bottom of the skillet. Tilt the skillet all around so that the batter swirls to coat the base thinly (try to make sure the center remains about 1/2 inch thick). Cook undisturbed for about 3 minutes until the appam is golden brown on the underside, and the edges lift easily.

7.   Flip the appam over with a spatula, and cook, but don't brown other side (about 1 minute more). Transfer to a platter, cover with parchment paper and keep warm in an oven until the entire batch is made.

8.   Serve hot with coconut milk sweetened with sugar.

Spicy Scones with Tomato Chutney Recipe

Time: 40 minutes

Yield: 4 servings

Although this recipe isn't strictly Indian, it uses an Indian style taste in a more Western breakfast to keep you satisfied in the morning.

Ingredients:

1 cup all-purpose flour

1 teaspoon baking soda

1 teaspoon salt

1 tablespoon ground mix of roasted cardamom, cloves, cinnamon, pepper

1/2 cup ghee

2 teaspoons grated fresh ginger

1 teaspoon cayenne pepper

1 tablespoon fresh dill, chopped

2 large eggs, beaten (divided)

4 tablespoons buttermilk

1 tablespoon carom seeds

10 oz. tomato Chutney

Directions:

1. Preheat the oven to 350° F. Line 2 baking sheets with parchment paper.
2. Sift together the flour, baking soda, salt, cayenne pepper, roasted spices and 1/2 tablespoon of the carom seeds into a large bowl.
3. Rub the ghee into the flour until the mixture resembles coarse breadcrumbs.
4. Add the grated ginger, dill, and the liquid ingredients – one beaten egg and all the buttermilk. Knead into soft dough.
5. Roll out on a floured surface to about 3/4ths of an inch thick. Cut into 1 1/2 inch scones using a cookie cutter. Make about 18 -20 scones.
6. Place on the lined baking sheets.
7. Whisk the remaining egg with a tablespoon of water. Brush the top of each scone with the egg mixture using a pastry brush, then sprinkle with carom seeds.
8. Bake for 10-15 minutes, until puffed and golden brown on top. Remove from oven and cool on a wire rack.
9. Split each scone in half and spread a layer of tomato chutney and put the halves back together. Serve warm as an accompaniment to tea.

Baked Beet Samosas

Time: 45 minutes
Yield: 4 servings

Samosas have spread in popularity from the Indian subcontinent and are now a food that's consumed all over the world. These Baked Beet Samosas go great as a snack or as a side to a healthy lunch.

Ingredients:

2 tablespoons butter or ghee, plus a bit more for brushing

1/2 teaspoon fennel seeds
1/4 teaspoon mustard seeds
1/2 cup finely chopped shallots
1 clove, minced garlic
1 teaspoon ground coriander
1 teaspoon salt, divided
1/2 teaspoon cayenne pepper, or to taste
1 cup boiling potatoes, cooked, peeled, and diced
1/2 cup beetroot – cooked peeled and diced
1 large puff pastry sheet

Directions:

1. Preheat oven to 400° F. Line a baking sheet with baking paper.

2. Heat the butter or ghee in a large sauté pan over medium heat, then add the mustard seeds and let them splutter (about 30 seconds).

3. Add the shallots and garlic, sauté 2 -3 minutes or until the onion is translucent. Stir in the fennel seeds, ground coriander, cayenne pepper and salt; cook about 30 seconds until fragrant.

4.   Add the potatoes and beetroots and mash slightly with a fork. Cook for 3 to 4 minutes for the flavors to blend. Remove from heat and cool for few minutes.

5.   Thaw the puff pastry sheet, unroll it and cut into 6" squares with a pizza cutter. Prick all over with a fork to prevent the pastry from puffing up.

6.   Place 2 tablespoons of the potato filling into the center of each puff pastry square. Brush the edges of the pastry sheet with a little water. Fold one corner over the opposite corner form a triangle and press the edges to seal. Brush both sides with a little butter or ghee and place on the lined baking sheet.

7.   Bake for 10 to 15 minutes or until lightly browned and crisp. Serve hot.

Kedgeree

Time: 1 hour
Yield: 4 servings

Kedgeree is a dish that is a staple in Indian culture. It's simple but hearty taste is something that can appeal to not only people in India, but all over the world.

Ingredients:

1 1/2 cup long grain white rice, washed and drained
3 cups water
1 tablespoon ghee
1 teaspoon cumin seeds
1 fresh tomato, diced
1 medium red onion, minced
1 green chili seeded, split lengthwise
1 tablespoon curry powder
2 teaspoons turmeric powder
1/2 cup vegetable stock/water
2 tablespoons Greek yoghurt
14 oz. chicken breasts, diced
2 cups soy granules
minced coriander for garnish
1 teaspoon lemon juice

Directions:

1. Mix the rice and 3 cups of water in a crock pot or heavy saucepan. Bring to a rolling boil and then simmer on low heat for 15-20 minutes until the rice is softened. Remove from flame and keep covered for 10 more minutes to let the rice cook in the steam.

2. Soak soy granules in water for 5 minutes, drain and press out excess water. Set aside.

3. Heat ghee in a large, deep pan until very hot. Add the cumin seed and sauté until they start to brown. Add the green chilli and sauté till the chilli whitens. Add the turmeric and onions. Fry until the onions are soft.

4. Add the diced tomatoes and vegetable stock, curry powder, soy granules and diced chicken breasts. Cook covered for 4-6 minutes, stirring occasionally until the mixture thickens.

5. Turn down the heat, and then add the cooked rice and Greek yoghurt.

6. Serve hot, garnished with chopped coriander and a dash of lemon juice.

Chicken Biryani

Time: 1 hour 20 minutes
Yield: 4 servings

If you've ever been to an Indian restaurant, you're bound to have seen Chicken Biryani on the menu. Here's a recipe so you can make it yourself.

Ingredients:

For chicken:

4-5 chicken breasts, diced
1 teaspoon ginger garlic paste

1 teaspoon salt
1/2 teaspoon biryani masala (available at Indian stores)
1/2 teaspoon cayenne pepper
1 teaspoon oil, plus more (3-4 tablespoons) for frying

For rice:

3 quarts water
1 teaspoon salt
10 green cardamom pods, whole
2 cloves, whole
1/4 teaspoon whole allspice
1 teaspoon ground coriander
1 bay leaf
2 Cups long grained white rice

For onions:

2 medium red onions julienned
2 green Serrano chilies, deseeded, finely chopped
1/2 teaspoon ginger garlic paste
1 teaspoon garam masala
1/4 teaspoon salt

For assembly:

Salt, to taste
3 tablespoons mint, minced

2 tablespoons pistachios, coarsely chopped
A few drops cardamom extract.

Directions:
1. Prepare the chicken – wash and pat dry. Mix together the ginger garlic paste, salt, biryani masala, cayenne pepper and oil to make a thick paste. Place the paste and chicken pieces in a Ziploc bag and rub the outside of the bag to coat the chicken. Keep aside.

2. In a large, thick bottomed crock pot, add the water, and all the ingredients for the rice. Bring to a boil and then reduce heat and cover, cook for 10 minutes. Drain the excess water (save 1 cup).

3. While the rice cooks, heat 3 tablespoons of oil in a large cast iron skillet over high heat. Add the chicken pieces. Stir fry the marinated chicken pieces for 5-6 minutes, until well browned and crusty.

4. Place the chicken in a separate bowl, and put the skillet back on medium heat. Then add the onions and sauté for 10-12 minutes until the onions caramelize. Add the chopped serrano chilies, ginger-garlic paste, garam masala, and salt. Cook for 30 seconds to a minute. Remove from heat and keep aside.

5. To prepare the biryani, remove half the rice from the crock pot, layer the mint and pistachios on top. Then layer half the onions and chicken. Add the rest of the rice and top with the remaining chicken followed by onions. Mix the cardamom extract with the reserved cooking liquid from the rice, and then pour it over the rice. Cover and cook on medium to low heat for 10 – 15 minutes till the rice is tender. Remove from flame; keep covered for 10 minutes for the rice to cook further. Stir to mix, serve hot.

Haleem

Time: 3 hours
Yield: 5 servings

Haleem is a dish that may be odd to look at, but tastes great when cooked properly. The key with Haleem is the consistency of the dish. You want something that's not too liquid and isn't too solid either. It should be able to hold its form when put into a separate plate.

Ingredients:

1/2 lbs ground chicken
4 tablespoons cooking oil
2 cups broken wheat
2 tablespoons barley
1/4 cup chick peas, drained
1 teaspoon split green chilies, deseeded, finely chopped
1 tablespoon French green lentils
1 tablespoon pigeon peas
1 cup red onion, finely sliced
2 teaspoons haleem masala, or to taste
1 tablespoon fresh cilantro, minced
1 teaspoon fresh lemon juice,

Directions:

1. Clean and wash the lentils and barley and soak in water for 2 hours. Wash the broken wheat and soak separately for 30 minutes.

2. In a sauté pan fry the red onion in oil until golden brown. Add the ground chicken, two teaspoons haleem masala and cook for 5 -7 minutes.

3. To a large, thick bottomed pot, add the soaked lentils, broken wheat and ground chicken mixture. Add 6 cups of water, then bring to a boil on medium to high heat, then cover

and simmer, stirring often until the meat and pulses are tender, (20 – 30 minutes).

4.   Serve hot, garnished with chopped fresh cilantro, chopped green chilies and fresh lemon.

Sprouted Mung Chaat

Time: 45 minutes plus 2 hours for soaking
Yield: 6 servings

Chaat is a word that the South Asian subcontinent uses for a variety of snacks, mostly using chick peas or other types of beans. This chaat uses mung beans for a great side dish or snack.

Ingredients:

2 1/2 cups sprouted mung beans, washed and drained
2 teaspoons canola oil
1 inch cinnamon stick
1 bay leaf

4 cloves, whole
1 onion, finely chopped
2 cups tomato puree
2 tablespoons tomato paste
1 green chili peppers – finely chopped
2 teaspoons ginger, flaked
1 teaspoon brown sugar
Juice of 1 lemon
1/2 teaspoon ground paprika
Salt, to taste
2 tablespoons chopped mint
2 cups potato chips, plain, salted
1/2 teaspoons spoon chaat masala (optional)
2 tablespoons fresh grated coconut (optional)
Lemon wedges, to garnish

Directions:

1. Heat the canola oil in a large pan.

2. When hot, add the cinnamon stick, cloves and the bay leaf and stir for about half a minute till they crackle.

3. Add the finely chopped onion into the spices and fry till golden.

4. Add the tomato paste and tomato puree, sprouted mung beans, flaked ginger and chopped green chili peppers.

Cook on medium heat for 7 – 10 minutes till the mung beans are cooked but still retain a crunch.

5. Add the brown sugar, salt and a pinch of ground paprika and stir well. Sprinkle the chopped mint on top.

6. To serve, spoon out the hot mixture in a shallow bowl, sprinkle a handful of crushed potato chips, followed by a teaspoon of chopped fresh mint and fresh grated coconut. Sprinkle a pinch of the chaat masala (optional) for added zing. Garnish with lemon wedges.

7. Serve hot as starter or as a side dish to flat breads.

Quick Indian Butter Chicken

Time: 1 1/2 hour
Yield: 6 servings

Butter chicken is another dish that's found at almost every Indian or South Asian restaurant and is extremely popular for a reason. The creamy and spicy taste is one that many try to mimic, but few can accomplish.

Ingredients:

1 pound skinless, boneless chicken breast, cubed
3/4 cup butter, divided
1 onion, ground to a paste
2 teaspoons ginger-garlic paste

1 (15 ounce) can tomato paste
1 can diced tomatoes
3/4 cup half and half
1 1/2 teaspoons salt
1 teaspoon ground red paprika
1 teaspoon roasted ground cumin
1 teaspoon garam masala
1 tablespoon tikka masala
1 1/2 tablespoons almond meal

Directions:

1. Preheat the oven to 375° F. Marinate the chicken cubes in a mixture of 1 tablespoon butter and tikka masala for 20 minutes.

2. Meanwhile in a deep skillet, melt most of the butter (save a tablespoon). Add onion paste, ginger-garlic paste, garam masala, ground cumin, red paprika, tomato paste, and diced tomatoes. Cover and simmer for about 10 – 12 minutes, stirring often till the gravy starts to thicken.

3. Place the marinated chicken cubes evenly on the baking sheet and bake for 10 minutes, or until the chicken is cooked through and juices run clear.

4. Add the baked chicken to the gravy and simmer for 10 minutes.

5. Remove from flame, stir in the half and half and almond meal.

6. Serve hot, with a dollop of remaining butter and rice or Indian bread.

Vegan Palak Paneer (Tofu in a Mild Spinach Gravy)

Time: 1 hour
Yield: 4 servings

Palak Paneer is a tasty dish that uses spinach and paneer (an Indian cheese) to satisfy taste buds everywhere. However, for your friends who follow a vegan lifestyle, use tofu and this recipe will be a hit.

Ingredients:

4 ounces tofu
2-3 bunches baby spinach (about a pound)
1 tablespoon vegetable oil

1 clove garlic minced
1-Inch fresh ginger, flaked
1 white onion
1 can diced tomatoes, drained
1/2 teaspoon ground cumin
1 teaspoon ground coriander seeds
1 bay leaf
1/4 cup soy /almond milk
Juice of 1 lemon
1/2 teaspoon fresh ground pepper
Salt to taste

Directions:

1. Drain and press out excess liquid from the tofu. Cut into 1 inch cubes.

2. Boil water in a large saucepan, add the spinach and leave it there for half a minute till the spinach wilts. Drain and mince.

3. In a sauté pan, heat some vegetable oil on medium, add the tofu cubes, and sauté till pale golden (do not brown). Set aside in a separate bowl.

4. Place the pan back on heat; add the onion, ginger and garlic. Sauté till the onion is translucent, about 2-3 minutes. Add the ground cumin, ground coriander seeds, the bay leaf

and stir till fragrant (about a minute). Add the diced tomatoes and simmer, covered for 4-5 minutes.

5. Add the minced spinach, tofu, salt, pepper and lemon juice. Stir well to mix

6. Remove the bay leaf. Drizzle the soy/almond milk on top.

7. Serve hot with naan or other flatbread.

Kerala Coconut Pork Curry

Time: 1 hour 15 minutes

Yield: 6 servings

This coconut pork curry is one that will have you wondering the limits of Indian food. There's nothing better than being surprised by your food.

Ingredients:

1 pound pork tenderloin, cut into 1 inch slices

Salt and pepper to taste

1 tablespoon coconut oil

5 shallots, peeled and quartered

1 inch ginger root, flaked

2 cloves garlic, chopped

2 tablespoons tomato paste

1 (10 ounce) can coconut milk

1 cup water

2 star anise

1/8 teaspoons cardamom seeds

2 bay leaves

1 teaspoon salt

1 carrot, peeled and diced

1 teaspoon fresh ground pepper

Directions:

1.	Rub the pork tenderloin pieces with salt and pepper.

2.	Heat the coconut oil in a large sauté pan over medium heat. Add the pork and cook for 5-6 minutes on each side till the pork is browned. Drain and transfer to a bowl and set aside.

3.	Wipe out the skillet and place the pan back on flame. Add the quartered shallots, ginger flakes and garlic and sauté till fragrant, or about 5 minutes. Add the cardamom, star anise and bay leaves and stir for half a minute.

4.	Add the sautéed pork, diced carrots, tomato paste, coconut milk and water. Cover and simmer for about 40 -50 minutes, stirring occasionally, until the pork is cooked through. Fish out the bay leaf and star anise.

5.	Serve hot, with rice or appams.

Tandoori Turkey

Time: 1 hour, plus 2 hours to marinade
Yield: 4 servings

Everyone's heard of tandoori chicken. Well how about Tandoori Turkey? This turkey meal will have you remaking all your favorite Indian dishes, but with tweaks every time.

Ingredients:

4 skinless turkey drumsticks or thighs
3/4 teaspoon salt
1 teaspoon dried basil
1 teaspoon ground coriander
2 teaspoons desiccated, unsweetened coconut

1 teaspoon ground allspice
1 teaspoon smoked paprika
1/2 teaspoon turmeric
1 tablespoon tomato paste
1/4 teaspoons fresh ground black pepper
1 cup Greek yoghurt
Freshly squeezed lemon juice
1 tablespoon ginger garlic paste
4 tablespoons vegetable oil

Directions:

1. Wash and pat the turkey pieces dry. Make deep cuts in the meat with a sharp knife.

2. Mix together all the ingredients (salt through ginger garlic paste) and rub this marinade generously into the turkey pieces.

3. Refrigerate for 2 hours.

4. Preheat your electric or charcoal grill. Brush with oil and grill the marinated turkey drumsticks for 20 to 25 minutes, turning the drumsticks every 10 minutes to ensure uniform cooking until well browned.

Halva

Time: 30 minutes

Yield: 4 servings

Halva is a sweet Indian dessert that can be made in various forms, but always tastes great. It's light, has a unique texture, and will be one recipe that you'll decide you have to master.

Ingredients:

1/2 pounds whole wheat flour
1 cup granulated white sugar
11/2 cups water

1 cup ghee
1/2 teaspoon saffron
1/4 teaspoon nutmeg
1 tablespoon raisins
Chopped pecans

Directions:

1. Heat ghee in a deep sauté pan. Add the whole wheat flour and roast on medium heat, stirring often until it becomes a pale brown.

2. Bring 1 1/2 cups of water to a boil in a separate vessel, and slowly pour into the flour mixture, stirring continuously to break up any lumps. Cook for 3-4 minutes till the mixture starts to thicken.

3. Stir in the sugar, saffron and nutmeg; cook for 2 minutes till the sugar dissolves.

4. Cool slightly, serve with raisins and chopped pecans.

Date Kheer (Indian Rice Pudding)

Time: 1 hour
Yield: 6 servings

Kheer is another dessert that's coveted by many around the world. Recently, you'll even see rice pudding in the desserts made by different companies at your local grocery store. However, there's nothing quite like making this for your friends and surprising them with an authentic kheer bowl.

Ingredients:

1/2 cup Basmati rice, washed and drained
2 tablespoons dates, pitted
2 tablespoons ghee
1/2 teaspoon saffron extract
1/2 teaspoon ground cinnamon
6 cups milk, divided
2 tablespoons suconat
1/4 cup slivered almonds, toasted
1/4 cup thinly roasted cashew nuts, finely chopped

Directions:

1. Puree the pitted dates in a food processor with a little milk to get a smooth paste.

2. Heat ghee in a large saucepan over medium heat; add rice and toast, stirring frequently till the rice gets a pinkish tinge (about 3 minutes).

3. Add milk, and cook, on medium heat, stirring occasionally, (keep a close watch; milk tends to boil over) until the rice is cooked (about 30 minutes).

4. Add date paste, almond slivers, most of the chopped cashew nuts, and suconat, and cook, stirring often for about 5 minutes, till the mixture thickens.

5. Serve hot or cold, garnish with chopped cashew nuts.

Gulab Jamun

Time: 1 hour, 15 minutes
Yield: 4 servings

Gulab Jamun are a personal favourite of mine. They may not be the healthiest, but when you bite into one, the feeling is hard to describe.

Ingredients:

Dough ingredients:
2 cups milk powder (with no added sugar)
1/2 cup bleached white flour
1/3 cup semolina flour
1/2 cup ghee

1 cup full fat milk
1/2 teaspoon baking soda
Ghee or canola oil for frying
1/8 teaspoon salt

Syrup ingredients:

3 cups water
1 1/2 cups sugar
1 pinch ground clove

Directions:

1. Mix the dry ingredients – milk powder, semolina flour and baking soda in a bowl.

2. Make a well in the center and add the ghee to the dry ingredients. Rub into the flour.

3. Slowly add the milk and mix till a soft dough forms. Do not over mix. Cover with a moist kitchen towel till the syrup is made.

4. To make the syrup, bring the sugar and water to a boil in a heavy sauce pan. Boil vigorously for a minute, and then reduce heat to just keep the syrup warm.

5.   Heat oil in a wok or deep fryer. Roll out the dough into a 1/2 inch thick rope. Cut off 1 inch pieces with a knife and roll into small ovals.

6.   Fry the balls slowly over medium heat, turning once or twice till they are fried uniformly to a rich brown. Drain and add the hot balls to the warm syrup. Soak them for about 10 minutes till they expand in size and the syrup is absorbed into the center of the balls.

7.   Serve warm or cold, with syrup.

Kulfi

Time: 25 minutes + freezing time
Yield: 4 servings

Kulfi is an Indian equivalent to ice cream. It's a bit different when it comes to texture, but try cooling off with these one day and you'll feel like you're in the streets of Mumbai.

Ingredients:

2 cups full fat milk
3/4 cup evaporated milk
1 tablespoon Dulce de Leche
2 teaspoons almond extract
3/4 cup caster sugar
Candied nuts, coarsely chopped

Directions:

1. In a heavy bottomed saucepan, mix together the milk, evaporated milk, Dulce de leche and caster sugar. Bring to a boil.

2. Reduce heat and let the mixture simmer for 15 minutes till the mixture thickens. Stir frequently to prevent the mixture from browning at the base.

3. Remove from flame and allow it to cool for about 15 minutes.

4. Pour into ice cream candy molds and freeze overnight till firm (or pour into a shallow pan and cut into bars).

5. To unmold, dip the molds in warm water for few seconds.

6. Garnish with candied chopped nuts.

Strawberry Lassi with Cherry Liqueur

Time: 5 minutes
Yield: 2 servings

Lassi is a yogurt drink that has been made for ages in the South Asian subcontinent and has been used to cool down on those blistering summer days. Add a bit of flavor with some liqueur or other methods and this might become a regular in your fridge.

Ingredients:

1 cup plain yogurt
1/2 cup half and half
1 cup fresh strawberry crush
2 teaspoons cherry liqueur
1/4 teaspoon salt

Directions:

1. Pulse the strawberry crush and yoghurt in a blender or food processor till smooth.

2. Add the cherry liqueur, half and half and salt; give a few quick pulses. Refrigerate for a couple of hours (optional).

3. Process the icing sugar in a food processor. Before serving, dip the rim of the glass in the powdered sugar, pour in the lassi. Serve chilled.

Chai Tea

Time: 10 minutes
Yield: 3-4 servings

Chai is a tea that is served before, after, and during so many meals that it's hard to find a time when someone's not drinking chai in an Indian household. Try the recipe once and you'll soon realize why.

Ingredients:

8 whole cloves

3 pods cardamom, crushed

1/4 teaspoon ginger powder

2 whole black peppercorns

1 inch stick cinnamon

3 cups water

1 tablespoon strong leaf tea

1 tablespoon vanilla sugar (or to taste)

Whole milk, hot, to taste (optional)

Directions:

1. Bring water to a boil in a small saucepan. Add the spices (cloves, cardamom, ginger powder, peppercorns and cinnamon) and boil for a minute. Remove from heat and allow the spices to steep for 5 minutes.

2. Strain and put back on heat. Add the vanilla sugar, and bring the mixture to a boil. Add the tea, immediately remove from heat and keep covered for 2 minutes.

3. Once spices have steeped, return pot to the stove and bring to a boil. Strain the tea leaves and discard. Add hot milk, to taste, if you like.

4. Serve hot.

Roasted Eggplant and Garlic Hummus

Time: 15 minutes
Yield: 12 servings

Here's another hummus recipe, since when it comes to hummus, you can never have enough. For those who bemoan the supposed lack of flavor in hummus, here's a recipe to ensure that they can happily enjoy a more flavorful hummus.

Ingredients:

1 eggplant, cut into 1/2-inch slices
2 tablespoons olive oil

2 garlic cloves, minced

1 (15 ounce) can white kidney beans, drained

1/2 teaspoon cayenne pepper

1/2 teaspoon salt

3 tablespoons olive oil

Directions:

1. Preheat oven to 350 degrees F. Lightly grease a baking sheet.

2. In a bowl, place eggplant, garlic, and oil. Toss until eggplant is completely coated.

3. Spread out eggplant on baking sheet and bake for 20 minutes.

4. In a food processor, add eggplant, oil, pepper, beans, and salt and pulse until smooth. Serve with pita chips or vegetables.

Part 2

Green Onion Bhurji

Ingredients
4 small bunches of green onions (onion bulbs with the leaves on) 3 eggs
1 teaspoon chilli powder
1/2 teaspoon Turmeric powder Salt
Oil

Method
Clean the green onions and cut the onion bulbs from the green leaves and chop the bulbs finely. Keep aside
Chop the leaves finely.
Take oil in a wide mouthed pan and saute the chopped onion bulbs for some time till they become soft.
Add the chopped leaves and mix well.
Close with a tight fitting lid. Decrease flame and let it cook till the leaves become soft.
After the leaves get cooked thoroughly, add chilli powder and turmeric powder.
Mix well.
Beat the eggs and add to the pan. Mix the whole mixture well till the eggs get cooked and the mixture is dry.
Add salt to taste. Serve piping hot.
Note : Do not add any water to the onion leaves. They should cook in their own juice.

Mysore Bonda

Ingredients
1 cup All purpose flour
2 Green chilies (finely chopped) 1 small onion (finely chopped) 1 big spoon full of rice flour Sour curd (to make the batter) Salt to taste
A pinch of baking soda
Chopped coriander leaves (optional)
Method
Mix all the above ingredients using the curd to a bajji dough consistency. Keep this aside for 3 hrs.
Heat some oil in a frying pan. When the oil is hot enough, drop the batter in oil and deep fry them till golden brown. Serve hot with green chutney or ketchup.
Make sure the curd is sour enough. These bondas are very crispy and tasty too.

Dahi Wada

Ingredients For the wadas
Udad dal (Black gram dal) 1 cup
Mung dal (Green gram dal) 1/4 cup Salt to taste
Method for Wadas
Soak the two dals for 7-8 hours or overnight. Grind it to a smooth paste.
Add salt to taste.

Heat oil for deep frying in a kadahi and add spoonfuls of dal batter and fry until the wadas are golden brown.

Drop the hot wads in a bowl of cold water and leave for about 3-4 minutes.

Take each wada out from water, squeeze the water out and set aside.

For the Dahi (yogurt)

Dahi (yogurt) 5 cups

(You can use homemade yogurt or low-fat yogurt from the market) Green chillies, chopped 1 tsp

Ginger grated 1/2 tsp curry leaves 7-8 Mustard seeds 1/4 tsp Asafoetida pinch

Salt to taste

Sugar 4 tsps (yogurt should taste little sweet)

Method for making dahi

Blend the yogurt with little water until it is smooth. Add sugar, salt, green chillies and ginger.

Make a tarka (seasoning) of mustard seeds, asafoetida and curry leaves and add to yogurt.

Keep the yogurt in refrigerator until it is chilled.

Serving the wadas

Arrange the squeezed wadas in a deep dish. Pour the yogurt on the wadas such that all the wads are covered well by the yogurt. Sprinle red chiili powder, roasted jeera powder and black salt (sanchal).Serve with sweet tamarind(imli) chutney.

Rasmalai

Ingredients Makes: 15 pieces

Shelflife: Refrigerator fresh 2-3 days.

4 Measuring cup milk for chenna (2% milk) 3 measuring cup milk for Ras

4 - 4 1/2 tbsp. sugar for Ras 1 cup sugar

3 cups of water

safforn, cardomom, pista, almonds lemon juice

Method

First keep the 3 cups of milk for ras to boil until it reamins 1 3/4 cup.

Bring 4 cups of milk to boil. Now to curdle the milk add lemonjuice to it stirring continously. Then drain it in athin muslin cloth or handkerchief.

Hold it covered with cloth in the running water.Drain the excess water by pressing the cloth there must not be water remaining.

In a pressure cooker take 3 cups of water and 1 cup of sugar. Take the chenna out of the cloth in a dish , mash it and make around 15 small size of balls out of it Toss that balls in the pressure cooker and bring two whistle.

In the mean time see the milk for ras may be ready.

Add the sugar for ras to it and add cardomon, pista, almond and safforn to it.Let it cool aside

As the pressure cooker is warm now open it take out the balls of chenna with the spoon ina dish and let the water drain by pressing it little and let it cook.

When the milk is cool add chenna balls to it. Refrigerate it. And it is ready to serve. Isn't it quick and easy
* while putting chenna balls inthe pressure cooker do not put one onthe other. Depending on the size of the pressure cooker I put 12 pieces at a time

Instant Dhokla

Ingredients
1 small bowl Besan 1 small bowl Water 1 teaspoon Salt
1/2 tablespoon Lemonjuice 1 tablespoon Oil
1 tablespoon Eno Fruit Salt
Tampering
1 teaspoon Mustard Seeds (rai) 2 Sliced Green Chillies
A few Curry Leaves 2 Tablespoon Sugar
2 tablespoon Lemon juice 1/4 cup Water
1 tablespoon Oil
2tablespoon Chopped Corinder 1 table spoon Grated Coconut
Method
Mix togather besan, salt, oil, lemonjuice and water.
In a pressure cooker or big vassle put 1 glass water and keep a mesh upside down. (so that water should not touch the dhokla pan)
Grease a baking dish (it should fit in the vassle or cooker)
Now add Eno and mix well and pour this mixture right away in the greased pan. Steam it for 20 minutes.

Prepare the tampring adding rai, greenchillies and curryleaves in hot oil. Mix togather water,sugar and lemonjuice and pour into tempring. boil it. Take out dhokla and cut into pieces. Pour the tapering mixture over it. Garnish with grated coconut and Coriander.

Matar Palak

Ingredients
1 bunch of spinach 1 cup of green peas
1 medium sizwd tomato 1 medium sized onion
1 medium sized boiled potato 3-4 green chillies
1 tsp. cumin seeds A pinch of asofetida
1 tsp turmeric powder Salt to taste
Method
Cut spinach leaves and wash them properly.
Boil the cut spinach for 10 minutes in a very little amount of water.
Allow to cool for sometime.Grind thecooled spinach alongwith the greenchillies to a fine paste.
This paste must be semiliauid.
Chop onion and tomatoes into small pieces. Cut the boiled potato into evenly shaped cubes.
Heat oil in a pan.Add the cumin seeds and asofetida. Add the onions,peas and tomatoes.

Fry for 2-3 mins. Add the potato cubes and allow to cook on medium flame for 5 mins.

Once the onions and tomatoes are cooked, add the spinach-chilli paste to the above.

Add turmeric powder and salt to taste.

Simmer it for 10 mins. Tastes good with rotis/parathas.

Aloo Mutter

Ingredients

1 cup green peas

2 medium size potatoes 2 medium size tomatoes

1 Pod Garlic (about 15-20 Pieces) 1/2 cup Green Coriander leaves

2 Green chilies

1 small onion Salt to taste

Pinch of Turmeric

Method:

Grind Garlic, Coriander, tomatoes, green Chillies, onion, salt, turmeric. Heat oil in cooker. Add ground Masala and roast till oil separates

Add potatoes pieces, and green peas and mix properly Add water and pressure cook. Serve with chappaties

Venn Pongal

Ingredients

Rice 2 cups

Toor Dal 3/4 cup

Coarsely crushed peppercorns 2 tsps Cumin seeds 1 1/2 tsp

Ginger 1 1/2 inches long cut into tiny bits Cashew nuts 5

Ghee 3 tsps

Method

Cook the rice and dal together either in a pressure cooker or in a vessel directly on the stove. The two should be cooked till soft.

In a seperate kadai add the ghee and when it is hot fry the cashew pieces in it. When the pieces turn brown add the crushed peppercorn and the cumin.

When they splutter add ginger and fry.

Add the cooked mixture of the rice and dal to it with salt according to your taste.Mix well. Add a teaspoon of ghee over it in the end before serving.

This can be eaten with coconut or onion chutney.

The rice and the dal can be cooked earlier and the rest of it just takes 5minutes.

Tamilian Kurma

Ingredients

1 cup shredded coconut 4 geen chillies

1 bunch coriander leaves

1 tsp poppy seeds (khusa khusa) gingerpaste

garlic paste

Grind all of the above ingredients to a fine paste with water. french cut beans carrots(sliced) lenghtwise peas(frozen will do) potatoes (cubed)

Method

Take oil in a kadai. Add jeera.And then add all the vegetables and let it boil. Add turmeric powder (a pinch), salt (2tsp), chillipowder (1tsp).

Add the ground ingredients and cook for about 15 mins. Add water if desired. Serve hot with rice.

Vegetable Korma

Ingredients

1 Cup Beans half cup Carrot 1 Potato

half cup Peas
half cup Ground coconut small piece Ginger
3 flakes Garlic
1 Onion
half tbs Cumin seeds
1 tbs Corriander powder few Corriander leaves half tbs Chillie powder half Lime
half tbs Turmeric powder
Take oil in a pan. Add the sliced onions.

After that add ginger, garlic, corriander powder, chillie powder, salt & fresh corriander leaves .
Fry it nicely.
Then add the vegetables & pressure cook till done.
When the vegetables are cooked add the ground coconut and little water to it & let it simmer for 5 minutes.
Squeeze lime to it & the veg korma is ready. Serve hot with chapatis.

Mixed Vegetable Kofta in Tomato Curry

Ingredients
For the Koftas you need
1/2 cup Frozen Corn 1/2 cup Frozen Peas
1/2 cup Green Beans cut in small pieces
1/2 cup Carrots cut in small pieces. 1 1/2 cup Gram Flour (Besan)
Salt to taste
1/2 Tsp..of Red chili Powder Pinch of Turmeric Powder
1 Tsp. of Mango Powder 1 Tsp. of Dhaniya Powder For the Tomato Curry: 1 Pound Fresh Tomatoes 2 Tsp. Tomato Paste
3/4 Cup of water Salt to Taste
1/2 Tsp. Red Chilly Powder 1/4 Tsp. Sugar
1/4 Tsp. Cinnamon Powder 2 pieces whole cloves
1 Tsp. Ground Ginger For Frying: Vegetable Oil
For Garnish :
Fresh Cilantro or Homemade Pannier
Method:

Parboil all the vegetables for 10 minutes. Let them cool for 20 minutes. Mix all the spices (except salt) and vegetables in a bowl.

Add salt to Gram Flour and add it slowly to the mixture. Keep on mixing it with your hand . Do not add water.

Add Gram Flour till you can shape them into small round soft balls. Use some oil in your palm of the hand to form the balls. Meanwhile heat some oil in the pan . See that the oil is not very hot. Keep Medium Flame.

Deep fry the Kofta balls.

Set them aside.

For the Tomato curry , I would highly recommend to cook the curry about 3 hrs before you serve.

Chop the tomatoes in small pieces.

Cook them with salt for about 15 minutes on medium flame. Add the Tomato paste. Keep on Stirring .

Add water and ginger and simmer for 2-3 minutes. Add the rest of the ingredients for the Tomato curry.

15 minutes before serving Put the Koftas in the serving dish and pour the Tomato Curry. Keep it in the oven at warm till you serve. Garnish with Fresh Cilantro or Paneer.

Chakali

Ingredients
3 cup rice flour 1 cup basan

1 stick butter (half cup)liquify 5,6 green chillies finely chopped

2 tsp coriander &cumin seed powder 1/2 tsp turmeric

2 tsp curd

1 tsp suger

salt to taste

Chakali utensil which is common for shev-papdi

Method

Mix rice flour & basan with all above interdients.add a little bit warm water and make a soft dough. (dough should be softer than the chapati dough.)

Grease the chakali utensil make chakali.

Deep fry in oilon midimum flame till golden brown in colour. Let it soak on paper.

serve with curd or butter.

Moong Soup With Paneer

Light and nutritious.

Preparation time : 5 minutes. Cooking time : 25 minutes.

Serves 6. Ingredients

¾ teacup moong

2 tablespoons finely chopped paneer 1 teaspoon cumin seeds

1 tablespoon mustard seeds

¼ teaspoon asafoetida 1 teaspoon lemon juice 2 pinches sugar

¼ teaspoon pepper powder

2 tablespoons ghee salt to taste

How to proceed

1. Soak the moong for a few hours. Add 6 cups of water and cook in a pressure cooker.
2. Blend the cooked moong in a blender. Strain.
3. Heat the ghee and fry the cumin seeds and mustard seeds. When they crackle, add the asafoetida and moong liquid.
4. Add the lemon juice, sugar, salt and pepper and boil for 2 minutes.
5. Add the paneer and cook for 2 minutes

Healthy Tomato soup

The ever popular tomato soup made in a healthier way.
Preparation time : 5 minutes. Cooking time : 25 minutes.
Serves 6. Ingredients

400 grams chopped tomatoes

½ teacup yellow moong dal 2 teaspoons butter

1 finely chopped onion

1 tablespoon cornflour or plain flour 1 to 2 teaspoons sugar

½ teacup warm milk salt and prepper to taste For serving fresh cream bread croutons How to proceed

1. Boil the tomatoes with the moong dal in 3 to 4 cups of water till cooked.

2. Blend in a blender and strain.
3. Melt the butter, add the onion and fry for 3 to 4 minutes.
4. Add the strained mixture.
5. Mix the cornflour with a little water and pour into the soup. Boil for 2 minutes, stirring ocassionaly.
6. Add the sugar, milk, salt and pepper.
Serve hot with cream and bread croutons.

Corn Soup with Vegetables

A soup with a Chinese touch.
Preparation time: 15 minutes . Cooking time: 30 minutes . Serves 6.
1 can (450 grams) cream-style corn 2 level tablespoones cornflour
1 teacup finely chopped mixed vegetables (cauliflower, carrots, cabbage, onions, french beans)
½ teaspoon Ajinomoto powder 3 tablespoons butter
2 tablespoons cheese
To be ground into a paste
25 mm. (1") piece ginger
4 cloves garlic
4 green chillies
For serving
chillies in vinegar and chilli sauce grated cheese

1. Mix the cornflour with 6 teacups of water. Add the paste, corn and Ajinomoto powder and cook in a pressure cooker until done.
2. Add the vegetables, butter and cheese and boil for a few minutes.

Serve hot with chillies in vinegar and chilli sauce or with grated cheese.

Green Peas Skin Soup

Preparation time: 10 minutes . Cooking time: 10 minutes . Serves 6.

6 teacups skin of green peas 1 tablespoon green peas

1 chopped onion

3 teacups skim milk 2 teaspoons butter

salt and pepper to taste

1. Heat the butter and fry the onion for 1 minute.
2. Add the green peas skin and green peas and cook for 3 to 4 minutes.
3. Add the milk and ½ teacup of water and cook in a pressure cooker till the first whistle.
4. Blend in a mixer.
5. Strain to separate the stock from the skin. Discard the skin.
6. Boil the stock for 1 minute.
7. Add salt and pepper.

Serve hot.

Health Information: This unusual soap gives the flavour of peas without the calories. Fresh green pea pods add fibre and Vitamins A and C to the soap. Fibre is called nature's broom because it helps sweep the products of digestion through the body and eliminates them.

Hara Nariel Ka Shorba

Coriander and coconut make a tasty combination.

Preparation time : 20 minutes. Cooking time : 10 minutes.
Serves 6. Ingredients

2 coconuts

6 teaspoons cornflour

1 teaspoon cumin seeds 2 tablespoons ghee

2 curry leaves

To be ground into a paste

2 tablespoons chopped coriander 2 small green chillies

1 teaspoon lemon juice

1. Grate the coconut. Add 6 cups of warm water and blend in a blender. Strain to obtain coconut milk.
2. Heat the ghee and fry the cumin seeds for 1 minute. Add the paste and curry leaves and fry again for 1 minute.
3. Mix the cornflour and coconut milk, add to the paste and boil for a few minutes.

Lentil and Vegetable Broth

Try out this unusual soup with moong dal stock.
Preparation time: 20 minutes. Cooking time: 20 minutes.
Serves 6 to 8. For the stock
2 tablespoones moong dal 2 onions
2 large tomatoes For the topping 1 chopped onion
½ teacup shredded cabbage
½ teacup chopped spinach
2 tablespoons baked beans or tomato ketchup 1 chopped tomato
1 tablespoon oil salt and pepper to taste grated cheese to serve

For the stock
1. Cut the onions and tomatoes into big pieces.
2. Add the moong dal and 6 teacups of water and cook in a pressure cooker.
3. When cooked, blend in a liquidiser and strain.

How to proceed
1. Heat the oil and fry the onion for 1 minute.
2. Add the vegetables and fry again for 1 minute.
3. Add the stock and boil for 10 minutes.
4. Add the beans, tomato, salt and pepper and give one boil.

Letil Soup

Preparation time: 10 minutes . Cooking time: 15 minutes . Serves 6.

¾ teacup masoor dal (washed) 3 sliced onions
4 cloves crushed garlic
½ teaspoon chilli powder 3 tomatoes
2 teaspoons oil salt to taste For serving
lemon juice

For garnish

1 tablespoon boiled rice

1. Heat the oil and fry the onions for 1 minute. Add the garlic and chilli powder and fry again for ½ minute.
2. Add 6 teacups of water, the tomatoes, masoor dal and salt and cook in a pressure cooker till the first whistle.
3. When cooked, blend in a mixer.
4. Boil for 5 minutes.

Serve hot with lemon juice and garnished with boiled rice.

Health Information: Pulses are an important source of protein containing twice as much protein as the same weight of cereals. The combination of cereals and pulses provides protein of high biological value.

Tum Yum Soup

The Thai soup with the intriguing flavour of lemon grass.
Preparation time: 15 minutes. Cooking time: 10 minutes. Serves 6.

6 teacups clear vegetable stock 1 green chilli, cut lengthwise
10 to 15 canned mushrooms, sliced
10 to 12 cauliflour florets (parboiled)
1 tablespoon roughly chopped lemon grass 2 pinches Ajinomoto powder (optional)
1 teaspoon lemon juice 2 to 3 drops oil
salt to taste

1. put the stock to boil.
2. Add the green chilli, mushrooms, cauliflower, lemon grass, Ajinomoto and salt and boil for 2 to 3 minutes.
3. Add the lemon juice and top with oil.

Serve hot with chillies in vinegar, soya sause and chilli sause.

Sweet Corn Soup

An old-time favourite.
Preparation time: 10 minutes. Cooking time: 30 minutes. Serves 6.

1 can (450 grams) cream style corn
½ teaspoon Ajinomoto powder
½ teaspoon soya sauce 2 tablespoons cornflour salt to taste
To serve
green chillies in vinegar chilli sause

1. Mix all the ingredients with 4 to 5 teacups of water.
2. Cook for 25 minutes.

Serve hot with chillies in vinegar and chilli sauce.

RAJMA CURRY

A favourable from the Punjab.

Preparation time : 20 minutes Cooking time : 20 minutes.

Serves : 6. Ingredients.

1 teacup red kidney beans (rajma) 2 onions, grated

1 teaspoon chilli powder 500 grams tomatoes

2 teaspoons sugar

3 tablespoons ghee Salt to taste

To be ground into a paste.

7 cloves garlic

7 green chillies 25mm. piece ginger How to proceed.

1. Soak the red kidney beans over night.
2. Next day, cook in a pressure cooker. Drain.
3. Heat the ghee and fry the onions for 2 to 3 minutes. Add the paste and chilli powder and fry again for 1 minute.
4. Add the cooked red kidney beans.
5. Cut the tomatoes intobig pieces, add 2 teacups of water and cook. When cooked, take out a thick soup through a sieve.
6. Add the tomato soup to the rajma mixture.Add the sugar and salt.

7. Cook for a few minutes.

Gujarati oondhiya cooked in the original style and served in an earthen pot with delicioius chutneys and sauces.

Preparation time : 40 minutes Cooking time : 60 minutes. Serves : 6 to 8. Ingredients.

750 grams (1 5/8 lb.) papadi

500 grams (1 1/8 lb.) kand (rataloo) 250 grams (9 oz.) potatoes

2 to 3 brinjals

1 teaspoon ajwain

1 teaspoon chilli-ginger paste 1/4 teaspoon soda bi-carb

1 to 2 tablespoons oil A few lettuce leaves Salt to taste

Green chutney, garlic chutney, sweet and sour sauce, sev and oil (optional) to serve

For the green chutney.

1 teacup chopped coriandder 4 green chillies

1 teaspoon lemon juice 1/2 teacup water

1/2 teaspoon salt

For the garlic chutney.

10 cloves garlic

2 teaspoons chilli powder 1/2 teacup water

1/2 teaspoon salt.

For the sweet and sour sauce.

1 teacup jaggery (gur) 1/2 teacup tamarind

1/2 teaspoon chilli powder 1/2 teacup water

Salt to taste

Chopped coriander for garnish

How to proceed.

1. String the papadi. Do not separate into two.
2. Peel the kand and cut into big pieces.
3. Cut the potatoes and sweet potatoes without peeling.
4. Make slits on the brinjals.
5. Mix all the vegetables. Apply the ajwain, chilli-ginger paste, soda bi-carb and salt. Mix thoroughly and apply the oil all over.
6. In a small earthen pot (matka), put a few leaves of lettuce at the bottom. Fill with all thevegetables and cover with the balance lettuce leaves.
7. Cover the matka, with an earthen lid and bake in a hot oven at 200 *C (400 *F) for 1 hour.
8. Alternatively, instead of cooking in a matka, wrap the vegetable mixture (without lettuce leaves) in aluminium foil and bake in a hot oven at 200 *C (400 *F) for 1 hour.
9. Serve with green and garlic chutneys and sweet and sour sauce, oil and seve.

For the green chuntey.

Blend all the ingredients in a liquidiser.

For the garlic chutney.

Blend all the ingredients in a liquidiser.

For the sweet and sour sauce.

Blend all the ingredients except coriander except coriander in a liquidiser. If too thick, add enough water to get the right consistency. Garnish with coriander.

MALAI KOFTA CURRY

A tasty kofta curry.

Preparation time : 30 minutes Cooking time : 40 minutes.

Serves :6. For the koftas.

100 grams green peas

100 grams cauliflower, finely chopped 100 grams french beans, finely chopped 100 grams carrots, finely chopped

250 grams potatoes, boiled andmashed 2 tablespoons bread crumbs

1 bread slice, soaked in water 1 teaspoon garam masala

1 teaspoon chilli powder

1 1/2 teaspoons lemon juice Salt to taste

Oil for deep frying

To be ground into a paste.(for the koftas)

9 cloves garlic

25 mm. (1") piece ginger

7 green chillies

For the gravy.

750 grams tomatoes

3 onions

4 cloves

2 small sticks cinnamon 1 tablespoon cornflour

1 teaspoon sugar

1 teaspoon garam masala 1 teaspoon chilli powder 4 tablespoons butter

Salt and pepper to taste

To be ground into a paste.

15 cloves
25 mm. (1") piece ginger
5 green chillies
For baking
1 tablespoon fresh cream 1/2 tablespoon grated cheese For the koftas.
1. Boil the peas.
2. Steam the cauliflower, french beans and carrots in a pressure cooker without adding water.
3. Add the vegetables and peas to the potatoes and make a dough.
4. Add 1 tablespoon of bread crumbs and the bread slice.
5. Add the paste, garam masala, chilli powder, lemon juice and salt and form into kofta balls.
6. Roll the koftas into the remaining bread crumbs and deep fry in oil to a golden brown colour. Keep aside.

For the gravy.
1. Put the tomatoes in hot water for 10 minutes. Remove and blend into a puree.
2. Blend the onions in a liquidiser with very little water.
3. Heat the butter, add the onions and stir fry for 5 minutes till light brown.
4. Then add the cloves, cinnamon and paste and fry again for 2 minutes.
5. Add the tomato puree and cook for 2 minutes.
6. Add 1 teacup of water and boil for 3 to 4 minutes.
7. Pour the mixture into a blender, add the cornflour and sugar and blend.

8.	Put to cook again and add the garam masala, chilli powder, salt and pepper and cook for 5 minutes.

How to proceed.

1.	Arrange the koftas in an ovenproof dish. Pour the gravy and fresh cream over the koftas.

2.	Sprinkle the grated cheese on top and bake or grill for 10 to 15 minutes in a hot oven at 200 *C (400*F) until the cheese melts.

Cheesy Sweet Jamuns

Makes about 24

150 gm puffed rice (murmura) - washed and soaked in water for 2 hours. 60 gm mawa

1/4 tsp baking powder Oil for frying Stuffing

90 gm Amul Cheese-grated 90 gm mawa

100 gm sugar

1 tbsp cashew nuts-chopped 2 tsp grated coconut

1 tbp raisins-chopped 1tsp chironji-chopped Syrup

200 gm sugar

3 cups water

1 tbsp milk

1/2 tsp cardamom powder 2 tsp rose essence

Silver foil for decoration

Method

Prepare syrup by boiling together the sugar and water. And milk and remove the scum as it surfaces. Boil till 3 cups of clear syrup are obtained. Remove from fire and flavour with essence and caedamom powder. Keep aside.

Cook the mawa for stuffing in frying pan till it is golden brown. Add the rest of the ingredients and mix well. form into small balls and keep separately.

Squeeze out the water from the puffed rice and mix it with the rest of the ingredients for Jamuns except oil. Knead well and from into as many balls as the number of stuffing balls you have. Flatten out the puffed rice balls on the plam of your hand and place a mawa ball on it. Fold over adn close sides to make an oval Jamun. deep fry on low fire till dark brown. Drain well and immerse in warm syrup for an hour. Serve warm decorated with silver foil.

Kofta Lajawab

Koftas
125 gm Amul Cheese - mashed 50 gm cornflour
1/2 tsp pepper powder Oil for frying

Gravy
250 gm onion - grated 200 gm tomatoes - pured

3 cm piece ginger - ground 1/2 tsp chilli powder
1/2 tsp garam masala 200 gm oil
3/4 tsp salt

Mix mashed cheese with cornflour and pepper. Knead well. Form into walnut sized koftas and deep fry till light brown. Drain and keep aside.

To make gravy, heat oil in a pan and brown onions. Add ginger and fry well.

Add tomatoes turmeric, red chilli and garam masala and fry on low fire till oil separates. Add water according to consistency of gravy required.

Correct seasoning. Boil for 5 minutes.

Add koftas and boil for a further two minutes. Serve hot with parathas or tandoori rotis.

Makes about 8

Beetroot Parathas

2 cups wheat flour
Water for kneading the dough Salt to taste
2 tbsp. ghee

Add two tbsp. ghee to wheat flour. Mix well, add enough water to knead to a soft dough.

For the stuffing:
2 cups beetroot, grated fine 4 medium sized onions
4 green chillies
2.5 cm. ginger 4 flakes garlic

1 tsp. garam masala powder Salt to taste
3 tbsp. ghee

Method

Grind all the ingredients, except garam masala powder, to a paste. Heat ghee in a vessel and fry the beetroot paste on a low flame. Cook covered, till the mixture is almost dry. Remove from heat.

Divide the paratha dough into small balls. Roll out each ball into a small puri, put a little beetroot filling in the centre and seal the edges. Roll out into parathas. Heat tawa, add some ghee and fry the parathas till light brown.

Badshahi Baigan

300 g. brinjals
1 cup curd
2 large onions, chopped 2 tomatoes, chopped
2 tsp. chilli powder
2 tsp. ginger-garlic paste 1 tsp. coriander powder
1 tsp. garam masala powder
1 tsp.coriander leaves, chopped 1/4 tsp. turmeric powder
1/4 tsp. cummin powder Salt to taste
1/4 cup ghee

For the garnish:

1 onion - sliced
1 tbsp. cashewnuts
1 tbsp. raisins

Method
1. Cut brinjals into 2.5 cm. thick slices.
2. Smear with salt and keep aside for 10 minutes.
3. Wash and squeeze dry.
4. Heat ghee, fry cashewnuts, raisins and sliced onion till golden brown. 5. Remove from ghee and keep aside.
6. Fry the brinjals in the same ghee till tender. Remove.
7. In the remaining ghee fry the chopped onions till transparent. 8. Add all the dry spices, ginger-garlic paste and chopped tomatoes and saute till the ghee floats on top.
9. Add curd, coriander leaves and salt. 10. Stir well. 11. Cook till the gravy thickens. 12. Add fried brinjals to the gravy and simmer for two minutes. 13. Sprinkle the garnish on top. 14. Serve hot with rice or parathas.

Red Tomato Gravy

Ingredients:
2 large juicy ripe tomatoes 1 large onion
1 small capsicum
1 tbsp. coriander leaves finely chopped 1 tbsp. cashews or peanuts
1 tsp. each ginger & garlic grated or crushed 1/4 tsp. cinnamon-clove powder
1/2 tsp. garam masala powder 3/4 tsp. red chilli powder
1/4 tsp. turmeric powder 1/2 tsp. sugar
salt to taste
2 tbsp. oil or ghee

Method:
Dry roast peanuts or cashews lightly. Dry grind coarsely. Semi puree tomatoes and capsicum together.
This should be done in a food chopper or grated. Chop onions very fine or run in a chopper.
Heat oil or ghee in a heavy pan.
Add ginger garlic and stir for a moment. Add onions and stir fry till light pink.
Add tomato capsicum puree, stir bring to boil.
Add all other masalas, salt, sugar and crushed nuts. Stir.

Add veggies at this stage. Mix.
Cover and simmer till gravy is thick and fat starts separating.
Garnish with coriander before serving.
Goes with: Vegetables like brinjals, baby corn, potato, stuffed baked capsicum, or cauliflower.
Makes: 2 cups

Green Gravy

Ingredients:
4 cups spinach chopped, washed and drained 1 cup bottle gourd grated
1 small onion finely chopped 1/2 tsp. ginger grated

2 tsp. wheat or millet flour 3 green chillies
1 tbsp. cheese grated (optional) salt to taste
1 tsp. lemon juice 1 pinch soda bicarb
1/2 tsp. cinnamon-clove powder 3 tbsp. oil

Method:

Take spinach in a large vessel, add gourd and soda. Toss to mix. Sprinkle 2 tbsp. water all over it.

Cover and put to boil on high, for 3 minutes. Cool in a plate or run under tap water to cool.

Put in a mixie, add chillies, flour and a few pinches salt. Run till semi-smooth.

Heat oil in a pan, add ginger, stir. Add cinnamon clove powder, and stir. Add onions, stir fry till light pink.

Add blended spinach mixture, all other ingredients except cheese Stir and allow to cook till thick or 3-4 minutes.

Add prepared vegetable at this stage. Allow to cook for 2-3 minutes more. Garnish with grated cheese before serving.

Goes well with: Veggies like peas, baby corn, french beans, potato chunks, etc.

Makes: 2 cups gravy (approx.)

White Gravy

Ingredients:
1 cup fresh curds 1/2 cup fresh cream
1 tsp. grated cheese or paneer 3/4 cup milk
1 tbsp. cashewnuts broken

1 tbsp. peanuts husked & lightly roasted
1 tsp. khuskhus seeds soaked in 2 tbsp. milk for 1 hour 3 green chillies
1 piece ginger
1 tsp. coriander finely chopped
1 slice dayold bread white 1 tsp. sugar
3-4 glazed or canned cherries (optional) salt to taste
1/5 tsp. cinnamon-clove powder 3 tbsp. ghee or oil

Method:

Grind together in a dry mixie, cashew, peanuts and bread. Grind together in a wet mixie, onion, ginger, chillies, khuskhus with milk. Heat fat in a heavy pan, add onion mixture, saute for 3-4 minutes.

Add curds and cook, stirring continuously till whiteness of curds disappears. Add milk, bring to a boil, add sugar, salt, dry mixture, spice powder, cream. Stir gently till boil resumes. Add vegetables, etc. at this stage.

Cook covered for few minutes till thickened. Garnish with grated cheese, coriander and cherries.

Goes well with: Paneer chunks, mixed vegetables with a few pineapples bits, potato and peas, etc.

Brown Gravy

Ingredients:
1 tomato grated or finely chopped 1 large onion cut in slivers
1 capsicum cut in thin lengths 1 tsp. garlic grated
1 tsp. ginger grated

1 tbsp. coriander leaves finely chopped 2 tbsp. tamarind water

1 tsp. wheat flour

1/2 tsp. red chilli powder 1/4 tsp. turmeric powder

1/2 tsp. dhania (coriander seed) powder 1/2 tsp. cumin seeds

3 pinches asafoetida salt to taste

3 tbsp. oil

Roast together and dry grind:

2 cardamoms

2 cloves

2 peppercorns

1/2 cinnamon stick broken 1 bayleaf

2 whole red chillies dry

Method:

Dry roast wheat flour to a light pink, stirring continuously. Keep aside. Heat oil, add onions, fry till well browned. Drain well by pressing, putting back oil in pan. Cool onions a bit. Grind in mixie. Keep aside.

In remaining hot oil, add cumin seeds allow to splutter.

Add asafoetida, capsicum, ginger, garlic stir fry for a minute.

Add all dry and ground masalas, flour, stir well.

Add tomatoes, tamarind water, salt, stir.

Simmer till gravy is thick and oil starts to separate.

Add prepared veggies and stir, keep cooking for 2 minutes.

Garnish with chopped coriander, serve with parathas, rotis, etc.

Goes well with: Chunky veggies like boiled baby potatoes with skin, boiled peas, chopped stirfried brinjal pieces. (For this, fry brinjals pieces in oil, drain, keep aside, adjust quantity of oil required, and continue by frying the onions.)

Besan Burfi

Ingredients:

1 c Besan 1 c Shortening 1 c Sugar 4 seeds Cardamom Nuts (optional)

Method:

Melt shortening in a pan. Turn down heat and add cardamom and Besan. Fry, stirring constantly to prevent burning until it has changed to a brown color and smells . (Test: a few drops of water sprinkled on it sputters instantly). Turn off the heat and stir in the sugar. Spread 1/2" thick onto a platter. Cut into diamond shapes after it has cooled down.

Raabdi

Ingredients:

* Whole Wheat/Plain Wheat flour -- 1 cup
*Sugar -- 6-7 tbsp
* Milk -- 4 cups
*Ghee/Unsalted Butter -- 4 tbsp
* Chopped Almonds -- 1 tbsp or to taste
* Chopped Pistachio nuts -- 1 tbsp or to taste<BR. strands * Raisins -- 1 tbsp or to taste

Method:
1. Melt un-salted butter in a pan on a mild flame for a few minutes to prepare ghee from butter.
2. Now add wheat flour to this
3. Stir till the flour is very very light brown in color. (At this point of time you can smell the aroma around!)
4. Add milk to wheat flour
5. Add sugar to mixture
6. Stir this mixture for 10-15 minutes on mild flame till its just a little bit thick (and NOT thick)
7. Add Almonds, Pistachio, Saffron (extremely good for winter)

Ras Malai

Ingredients:

Ricotta Cheese 2 lb. Half and Half 2 qts. Sugar 2 cups
Cardamon pods 5
Bay leaf 1
Vanilla 1 tsp.
Rose Water To taste (opt.)
Method
Mix 1.5 cups of sugar with the Ricotta cheese and bake it in a 400o F oven for about 1hr and 15 minutes in a flat dish

covered with aluminum foil. The cheese should have hardened and turned a pale brown.

Thicken the Half and Half by simmering over low heat for a long time. This is best done in a microwave; if a microwave is not available, do it over low heat and stir frequently. Thicken until the volume drops to around half of the origi- nal volume. Add the remaining 0.5 cup sugar, cardamon pods, bay leaf, vanilla and rose water (and any other flavouring that you may want) to the Half and Half. Heat for a few minutes. After the cheese has been baked, cut it into 1 inch squares and add to the hot thickened half and half. Cool for a few hours in the fridge.

Rasagulla

Ingredients:

Milk 1 gallon Lemon Juice 1 cup Sugar 1 cup
Method
Bring one gallon of milk to a boil. When boiling add one cup of either whiter vinegar or lemon juice. Turn the stove off. Milk should separate into whey and curd.

Pour into collander, leaving only the panir/curd. Leave curd in strainer until cold and dry. This will take at least an hour (you can leave it overnight).

Place curd in food processor and process for one minute. It should be soft but not sticky.

Form small balls from the curd. Using vinegar usually re- sults in about 80 to 100 rasagollas.

Bring one cup sugar and 3 cups water to a boil in a pressure cooker. Place 20-25 rasgoolas in syrup. Turn off the heat to place the cover on the pressure cooker. Turn heat on high. When cooker begins to whistle wait for a couple of minutes, then turn it off.

When pressure cooker depressurizes, remove cover and re- peat previous step with the rest of the rasgoolas. Do not use the same sugar syrup more than once.

Dum Arvi

Ingredients:
Arvi = 500gm Curd = 1 cup Salt to taste Oil for frying Sliced almonds for garnishing

Method:
Boil the arvi and peel the skin. Prick with fork, fry in oil, and drain. Heat2 tablespoon of oil in another container and add spices to taste (asafetida, chili powder, corriander powder,

salt, onion and ginger paste, and a table spoon water. Fry for sometime and then add curd and keep frying till it turns golden brown. Add fried arvi and 1/2 cup water and keep cooking on mild heat till it has almost got dried. Garnish with fresh corriander and sliced almonds and serve hot. Cooking time about 25 minutes and should be sufficient for 2-3 people.

Dum Aloo

Ingredients:

Oil 3 tbsp.
Bay leaf 1
Onion 1 Ginger 1/2 tsp. Garlic 1/2 tsp.
Cumin Seeds 1/2 tsp.
Turmeric 1/4 tsp.
Chili Powder 1 1/2 tsp.
Yogurt 2/3 tsp.
Salt 1/4 tsp.
Coriander powder 2 tsp.
Potatoes 1 lb.
Tomato 1
Capsicum 1
Method

Heat oil, add bay leaf and onion. Fry for 3-4 minutes. Add ginger and garlic and fry for another minute. Add mustard and cumin seeds.

The potatoes should be sliced, and the tomatoes and capsicum cut up. Add these, mix well, and cook for 4-5 min- utes, continuously stirring.

Sprinkle with turmeric, coriander and chili powder.

Beat the yogurt and blend into a smooth mixture. Add yogurt and salt.

Mix gently, cover and cook for about 10 minutes on low heat.

Matar Paneer

Ingredients:

6 paneer chunks about 1-1/2 x 1 x 1/2 inch each 1/4 cup oil 1 medium onion, chopped fine 1 tablespoon garlic/ginger paste, or 3 garlic cloves, mashed 1 piece fresh ginger, size of walnut, minced 1 large tomato, chopped

Dry Masala:

1/2 teaspoon ground coriander 1/4 teaspoon ground cumin 1/4 teaspoon red chili powder 1/4 teaspoon turmeric 1/2 teaspoon garam masala 1/4 cup water 3 cups fresh shelled green peas (or substitute 2 packages frozen) 1 tablespoon cashew nuts, ground to a paste with a bit of water Salt and freshly ground pepper to taste

Method:

Prepare the cheese chunks, and in a wok or heavy skillet fry them in hot oil until golden. Remove with slotted spoon and set aside to drain on a paper towel.
In the remaining oil sauté the chopped onion until it begins to turn brown. Do not scorch. Add the garlic/ginger paste and bhoona 2 minutes. Add the chopped tomato and bhoona 5 minutes to achieve a thick gravy. Add the dry masala and bhoona 3 minutes more. (NOTE: If the sauce is lumpy at this stage, puree it in a blender and continue.) Add 1/4 cup water, then stir in the peas. Add the paneer cubes and bhoona 2 minutes. Stir in the cashew paste, add salt, pepper. Serve at once. Serves 4 to 6 people.

Bhindi Masala

Ingredients:

1 pound (1/2 kg) okra (small) 2 onions, thinly sliced
2 tomatoes, chopped 1/4 cup oil
3/4 teaspoon paprika
1 teaspoon amchoor powder (or substitute fresh lemon juice)
1/2 teaspoon turmeric

salt and freshly ground pepper to taste 1 teaspoon garam masala

2 tablespoons chopped coriander leaves for garnish

Method:

1. Wash okra under running water and slice off the ends. Cut each in half. Set aside. Prepare onions and tomatoes. Set aside.

2. In a wok or heavy skillet heat the oil and sauté onions until translucent.

3. Add all spices except the garam masala and stir-fry 2 minutes. Add the tomatoes and bhoona * 1 minute. Add the okra and stir-fry 2 minutes. Cover and steam over medium heat until tender, about 12-15 minutes.

4. Spoon the okra onto a warm serving plate and sprinkle with the garam masala. Garnish with the coriander and serve while hot.

* Bhoona is a technique that is essential to Indian cooking. The bhoona technique means that the mixture is cooked over medium-high heat, with constant stirring to avoid scorching, until all liquids are reduced and the spices coat the meat like a paste. About 1/2 cup of water can then be added, the dish

covered, and a gravy created as the dish becomes liquified again. Serves 4-6 people.

Vegetable Jalfrasie

Ingredients

Onion 1 large
Green peppers 2
Tomatoes 2 large Broccoli 1/2 lb. Cauliflower 1/2 lb. Butter 4 tbsp.
Red Chili Powder 1 tsp. Turmeric 1/2 tsp.
Ginger 1 in. stick Garlic 3 cloves White vinegar 2 tbsp. Tomato puree 2 tbsp.

Method

Chop onion; cut green peppers, tomatoes, broccoli, and cauliflower into 1 in. cubes.
Melt butter and saute onion. Add all the remaining vegetables and stir-fry for about 5 minutes over medium heat.
Add the spices and vinegar. Stir in the tomato puree, and simmer for about 5 minutes. Season to taste with salt and fresh-ground pepper.
Dal radish Ingredients 1 cup toovar dal (soaked in water for one hour) 2 radishes 1 large tomato 1 large onion 1 tbsps. sambhar powder 1 tsp. jaggery 2 tbsps. finely grated coconut
A little mustard 2 sprigs of curry leaves 6 whole cashewnuts 2

tbsps. oil Salt to taste. MethodScrape and cut radish into round pieces. Heat oil in a kadai. Put in the mustard. When it splutters add chopped onion. Fry till golden brown. Mix chopped tomato, curry leaves, sambhar powder and the grated coconut. Keen frying for a few minutes. Add drained toovar dal and the radish slices. Add salt to taste and about two cups of water. Simmer on a slow fire till cooked. Serve hot with rice.

Rasam Masala

Masala Ingredients
Black Pepper 1 tbsp.
Chana Daal seeds 2 tbsp.
Coriander Seeds 2 tbsp.
Red Chillies 4-5
Asafoetida(optional) 1 tsp.
Coconut (grated) 3 tbsp.
Ghee 2 tbsp.
Masala Preparation
Roast black pepper, chana daal, coriander, and asafoetida. Add chillies when daal starts getting red.
If using dry coconut, soak it in a little water. Blend the daal mixture and coconut until the paste is fine. Keep aside.

Mangalore Rasam Powder

Ingredients:

Redchillies - 1 cup (broken intosmallpieces and tightly packed).

Dry coriander seeds - 1 cup Gram dhal - 2 tablespoons Oil - 1 tablespoon
Cumin seeds - 1 teaspoon
Fenugreek - 1/2 teaspoon (methi seeds)
Hing - a pea size lump or 1 teaspoon hing powder.
Curry leaves - 3 sprays.

Method:

Breakup the chillies along with the stalks into smaller pieces (toenable easier powdering). Heat oil in a kadai and fry on a slowfire, the hing and the fenugreek seeds till light brown in colour. Add coriander seeds, red chillies, cumin seeds, gram dhal andcurry leaves and fry for about five minutes on a slow flame tillit is well roasted and you get a lovely aroma. Removefrom flameand allow to cool. Powder fine and bottle it. This powder can be used for 2-3 months.

Use the chillies along with the stalks - as the stalks also have
thepotencyofthe chillies, and also provide fibre for the body).
***

Mangalore Rasam

(serves 6).

Ingredients

Tuvar dhal (thuvaram paruppu) - 1/2 cup. Tamarind - lime size.

Tomatoes - 2

Green chillies - 1

Rasam Powder - 3 teaspoons p73

Sugar - 2 teaspoon (optional) - 2-1/2 tsp. Salt - 1-3/4 teaspoon

Turmeric powder - 1/4 teaspoon Seasoning

Ghee - 1 teaspoon Red Chilli - 1

Mustard seeds - 1 teaspoon Black gram dhal - 1/2 teaspoon

Method

Pressurecooktuvar dhal with one cup of water and apinch of turmericpowderfor ten minutes - when cold, mash well. Soak tamarind in two cups of water for ten minutes, squeeze and strain outthe liquid. Boil tamarind water with turmeric powder, slit greenchilli, tomatoes (chopped) salt and sugar tillthe raw smell of tamarind disappears and the tomatoes are cooked. Add the masheddhal, two and a half cups of water, and the rasam powder andboil for five minutes till slightly thick. Add curry leaves and coriander leaves. Remove from fire.

Heatghee in a pan, add the mustard seeds, red chilli and black gramdhal. When mustard seeds splutter add hing powder- pour the seasoning over the rasam. Serve rasam hot with steaming rice and papads.

Sambar

(serves 6)

Ingredients

Tuvar dhal - 3/4 cup

Vegetables - 3 cups (like sambar onions, white pumpkin, chow-chow)

Tamarind - lemon size

Coriander leaves - 2 tablespoons Curry leaves - 1 tablespoon

Rasam powder - 2 teaspoon

Salt - 1-3/4 teaspoon - 2 teaspoons Sugar - 1-1/2 teaspoon (optional) Turmeric powder - 1/4 teaspoon Green chillies - 2-4.

Seasoning

Oil - 1 tablespoon Red chilli - 1

Mustard seeds - 1 teaspoon Black gram dhal - 1/2 teaspoon

Hing powder - 1/4 teaspoon

Method

Pressurecookdhal with one and a half cups of waterfor ten
minutes. When cold mash well. Soak tamarind in one cup of water,
for five minutes, squeeze well and strain out juice.

Cook vegetables in one and a half cups of water. When three-quarter cooked add slit green chillies, salt and sugar. Add tamarind water and simmer till raw smell disappears. Add mashed p73 dhal, rasam powder and curry leaves. Simmer till thick, add coriander leaves.

Heat oil in a pan, add mustard seeds, black gram dhal and red chilli. When mustard seeds splutter, add hing powder and pour the seasoning over the sambar. Serve sambar hot with rice and chips.

***

Cauliflower Curry

(serves 6)

Ingredients Cauliflower - 3 cups (in flowerets) Peeled and cubed potatoes - 2 cups Oil - 4 tablespoons Coriander leaves - 1 tablespoon Rasam powder - 2 teaspoon Cummin seeds - 1 teaspoon Salt - 1 teaspoon Sugar - 1 teaspoon Turmeric powder - 1/4 teaspoon Hing powder - 1/4 teaspoon Onion - 2 Green chillies - 2 Capsicum - 1 Ginger - 1 cm p73
Method:Chop all vegetables. Heat three tablespoons oil in a kadai, add the cummin seeds and hing powder. When the cummin seeds splutter add the onions, capsicum, green chillies and ginger into the hot oil and fry till the onion turns golden. Add tomatoes and fry till it becomes mushy. Add cauliflower, potatoes and turmeric powder, fry a bit, add salt, sugar and quarter cup of water. Cover and cook till the vegetables are cooked and the curry is dry. Add the rasam powder, coriander leaves and the remaining one tablespoon of oil-fry till you get a lovely aroma. Remove and serve piping hot with rotis or rice. (Plain potato curry can also be made the same way).

Sambar Masala

Masala Ingredients

Methi (Fenugreek) 1 tsp.
Chana Daal seeds 2 tbsp.
Coriander Seeds 4 tbsp.
Red Chillies 4-5
Asafoetida(optional) 1 tsp.

Coconut (grated) 3 tbsp.
Oil 3 tbsp.

Masala Preparation
Roast methi, chana daal, and asafoetida.
Add chillies when daal starts getting red.
If using dry coconut, soak it in a little water and blend the daal mixture and coconut until the paste is fine. Keep aside.

Vada

Ingredients

Moong Daal 1/2 cup Urad Daal 1/2 cup Onion 1
Coriander 2 tsp.
Green Chili 1
Chili powder 1/2 tsp. Salt 1 tsp.
Ginger 1 tsp.
Baking Soda 1/4 tsp.

Method
Soak urad daal and moong daal for 2-3 hours.
Grind daals into a coarse paste.
Add finely chopped onion, salt, coriander powder, chili powder OR green chili, ginger and soda. Mix well and set aside for 4-5 minutes.
Fry small spoonfuls of the mixture in hot oil.

Didir Onion Rava Dosa

Ingredients

one cup semolina/rava one cup maida
1/2 cup rice flour
4-5 green chillies finely chopped 3/4 inch ginger chopped fine
1 1/2 tspn jeera slightly crushed (enough to bring out its flavor) salt to taste
good pinch asafoetida 2-3 chopped onions
a bunch cashews oil to make dosas

Method

Mix rava, maida, rice flour together into a thick batter adding little water at a time so no lumps are formed. Mixing by hand is a good idea if you don't have a whisk or electric mixer. Add salt, crushed cumin asafoetida and leave in a warm spot for six to seven hours at least.

When ready to eat, spray a non-stick pan lightly with oil and warm.

Thin out the batter to the consistency where it can be drizzled onto the pan with a spoon. Drop chopped green chillies and ginger into batter.

Sprinkle some of the cut onions and cashews onto the pan and now continuing on low-medium heat, drizzle the batter such that there is a latice work effect. A lot of holes is just the thing. Dribble a bit bit of oil around it and when the edges start turning brown coax it off the pan with a flat, wide spatula and flip it over. Remove in a few minutes and make more.

For the plain rava dosa leave out the onions.

Didir Dosa

Ingredients

3 measures of rice flour 1 measure of urad flour

Method

Mix well so no lumps are formed. Salt to taste. Leave covered in a large pot overnight. Make thin crepes, preferably in non-stick pan.

Dosai

Ingredients

Rice 1 1/2 cups Urad Daal 1/2 cup Salt 2 tsp.

Method

Soak the rice and daal separately in slightly warm water for 2 - 8 hours.

Grind separately to a smooth paste and mix in a large vessel with salt. Mix thoroughly (use blender if possible).
Ferment for 12 hours.

Basic Curry Sauce

Ingredients

3 tablespoons vegetable oil or ghee (clarified butter)
1 medium onion - finely chopped
4 cloves garlic - peeled and sliced
1.5 inch piece root ginger - peeled and thinly sliced (it should look about the same volume as the garlic)
(optional) 2 mild fleshy green chillies - de-seeded and veined then chopped
half teaspoon turmeric powder
half teaspoon ground cumin seed
half teaspoon ground coriander seed
5 tablespoons plain passata (smooth, thick, sieved tomatoes, US = purée) or 1 tablespoon concentrated tomato purée (US = paste) mixed with 4 tablespoons water

Method

Heat the oil in a heavy pan then add the chopped onion and stir for a few minutes with the heat on high. Add the ginger, garlic and green chilli (if using). Stir for 30 seconds then put the heat down to very low. Cook for 15 minutes stirring from time to time making sure nothing browns or burns.

Add the turmeric, cumin and coriander and cook, still very gently, for a further 5 minutes. Don't burn the spices or the sauce will taste horrid - sprinkle on a few drops of water if you're worried.

Take off the heat and cool a little. Put 4 fl oz cold water in a blender, add the contents of the pan and whizz until very smooth. Add the passata and stir.

Put the puréed mixture back into the pan and cook for 20 - 30 minutes (the longer the better) over very low heat stirring occasionally. You can add a little hot water if it starts to catch on the pan but the idea is to gently "fry" the sauce which will darken in colour to an orangy brown. The final texture should be something like good tomato ketchup. Warning - it WILL gloop occasionally and splatter over your cooker, it's the price you have to pay!

Biryani

Indgredients: (serves 6)
2lbs Spring Lamb (cleaned and cut into medium size pieces)
4ozs Yougurt
4ozs Ghee
1lb Rice (washed)
4ozs Onions (sliced finely)
1oz Ginger & Garlic (equal amounts crushed) 1 Lemon
1oz Armonds (ground) 2 Cinamon sticks

4-6   Cardimons 1oz Milk

Qtr tspn Safron

2-3 Green Chilies Half tspn Black Zeera 2-3 Cloves

Half tsp Garam Masala

(equal amounts of Black Zeera, Cardimons & Cinamon sticks, with half amount of cloves) Salt to taste

Corriander and Fried Onions to Garnish Method:

In a large bowl mix the meat, yoghurt, almonds, chopped green chillies, ginger and garlic, salt, and ground garam masala. To the mixture add half a teaspoon each of chilli powder and termeric. Marinate for at least 4-6 hours in the fridge.

Fry the onions in ghee until golden brown and crisp. Drain away any excess ghee and then remove the onions and spread over a large plate. This should keep the onions crispy. Once they have cooled crush the onions with your fingers and add this to the marinated meat mixture.

In a large pan half fill with water and add salt, whole garam masala and one green chilli. Bring this to the boil and add the washed rice and cook until the water boils. Once the water has boiled drain the rice in a colander and rinse with a little cold water.

Grease the saucepan generously with ghee and transfer the meat mixture. Level the surface and now spread the rice evenly over the meat. Squeeze the lemon and pour the juice over the rice. Warm the milk and crush the safron into it. Pour the milf/safron mixture over the rice. Dot generously with ghee. To garnish spread the fried onions and corriander over the rice.

Cover the saucepan tightly. Allow to steam on high heat for about 10 minutes and then lower the heat and cook for another 1 and a half to 2 hours. Before removing the pan from the cookeer ensure that there is no moisture left in the meat. This can be checked by simply listening for a sizling sound. If there is no sizzling then the Biryani is ready.

Biryani is traditonally served with Mirch Salan and Yoghurt Chutney.

Double Ka Meetha (Bread Pudding)

Ingredients:

1 loaf bread (small) 1 lt milk
500 gms sugar
250 gms double cream 250 gms clarified butter
100 gms chopped and roasted cashewnuts 100 gms almonds (soaked and chopped fine) 10 gm saffron
5 cardamom powdered Method:
Cut each bread slice into four pieces. Fry them in clarified butter till golden brown. Make a sugar syrup by adding half a litre of water to the sugar and boil it for 15 minutes. Add the powdered cardamom and the saffron dissolved in milk to the sugar syrup. Boil milk until it is thickened.

Arrange the fried bread pieces on a flat tray and sprinkle the chopped nuts on them. Pour the sugar syrup, double cream and milk alternately over the bread pieces while they are still hot.

Refrigerate and serve as dessert. Eggs in a Spicy Cream Sauce 3 tbsps vegetable oil 2 oz onion, finely chopped 1" cube ginger, grated 1 fresh green chilli, finely chopped ½ pt single cream 1 tbsps lemon juice 1 tsp ground roasted cumin 1/8 tsp cayenne ½ tsp salt ¼ tsp garam masala 2 tsps tomato paste ¼ pt chicken stock 6-8 hard boiled eggs,halved 1 tbsp fresh coriander, chopped

Heat the oil over a medium heat in a large frying pan. When hot put in the onions. Stir and fry for about three minutes or until the peices are browned at the edges.

Put in the ginger and chilli. Stir and fry for a minute.Put in the cream, lemon juice, ground roast cumin, cayenne, salt, garam masal, tomato paste and chicken stock.Stir to mix thoroughly and bring to a simmer. Put all the egg halves into the sauce in a single layer, cut side up. Spoon the sauce over them. Cook over a medium heat for about five minutes, spooning the sauce over the eggs. Serve sprinkled with fresh coriander.

Indian Cream of Tomato Soup

1½ lb ripe tomatoes,chopped 1 tbsp chopped lemon grass 2 curry leaves
2" fresh ginger,peeled& chopped 1 tsp salt
4 fl oz water
4 fl oz single cream 1 pt milk
1 tsp ground roasted cumin seeds pinch ground black pepper pinch cayenne pepper
2 tsps lime or lemon juice
1 tbsp chopped coriander leaves

Put the tomatoes,lemon grass, curry leaves,ginger, salt and water into a saucepan and bring to the boil. Lower the heat, cover and simmer gently for 15 minutes.
Uncover, increase the heat and simmer more rapidly for another 15 minutes.Puree in a liquidiser then sieve. You should have about ¾ pt thick tomato juice.
Add the cream, milk, cumin seed, black and cayenne pepper and the lime or lemon juice. Stir together well and reheat gently without boiling.
Serve garnished with freshly chopped coriander.

Kadhi

1 cup buttermilk1/4 cup besan1 cup watersalt and chilli pd. to tastea pinch of Heeng (a MUST)a few kadhi patta 1/2 tsp. turmeric1 tsp. oil or ghee1/2 tsp. mustard seeds1/4 tsp. garlic pd.a little bit of minced gingerTo

make pakode for the kadhi you'll need:1/2 cup besansalt and chilli pd. to tastea little garam masala1/4 tsp. baking sodaoil to deep fryMake the pakode and keep them aside. Now mix the besan for the kadhi with the buttermilk. Add salt, ginger, garlic and chilli pd.to the same so that they mix thoroughly as well. now heat up the oil. Add the mustard seeds, kadhi patta, turmeric and heeng and then pour in the liquid. Add the water and let the whole thing simmertill the "kachcha" taste of besan is gone i.e. till the whole thing tastes as if" kadhi pak gayi hai". If the water has evaporatedby now do add more as now we'll add the pakode to the kadhiand boil the whole thing till the pakode get completely soaked.Making kadhi is not as difficult as it seems from the recipe butit might take you a little bit of practice to perfect the ART asit takes some instinct.

Bengan ka bhurta

1 fair sized egg plant3 medium onions , chopped3 medium tomatoes, chopped1/2 tsp. garlic pd.a little ginger, minced3 tbsp. oil1 jalapeno pepper, chopped1/2 tsp. amchur or anardanasalt and chilli pd to taste1 tsp. corriander pd.1/2 tsp. garam masalaPut the eggplant as is into the oven at 350

till its done. You'll know that its ready when the skin is all wrinkled and water seepsout of it. Peel and mash the eggplant and then "Bhagarofy" itwith all the ingredients. Make sure you "bhunofy" the whole thing really well. If you want you can even add some dry fruits to the stuffas well. Some QUICK sweet for a busy guy :

Halwa

1 cup cream of wheat (Sooji/Rawa, you can find that in the cereal section of the store)2 cups of water1 cup sugar1/2 cup unsalted butter or gheesome raisins and cashewsHeat up the butter at medium heat and add the cream of wheat to it. Let the c of w become golden pink and then add the water. Stir the whole thing quickly so that no lumps are formed. When the water more or less evaporates,add the sugar and the dry fruits. Once the consistency is right just eat it up. The whole thing should at most take you 15 minutes and it never fails - comes out perfect each time.

Toll House Pan Cookie

2 /14 cup all-purpose flour
1 measuring teaspoon baking soda 1 measuring teaspoon salt

1 cup butter softened
¾ cup sugar
¾ cup firmly packed brown sugar
1 measuring teaspoon vanilla extract 2 eggs
One 12-oz pkg. (2 cups) Nestle Semi-Sweet Real Chocolate Morsels 1 cup chopped nuts (optional)

Preheat oven to 375 F. In small bowl, combine flour, baking soda and salt; set aside. In large bowl, combine butter, sugar, bron sugar and vanilla extract; beat until creamy. Beat in eggs. Gradually add flour mixture; mix well. Stir in chocolate morsels and nuts. Drop by rounded measuring teaspoonfuls onto ungreased cookie sheets.

Bake: at 375 F.
Time: 8-10 minutes.
Makes: 100-2" cookies

Rasavangi

ingredients:Brinjal-big size 2nos, Toor dal - 1cup,Tamarind(imli)pulp -1 table spoon, turmeric powder 1/4 teaspoon, salt -to taste
For the paste:coriander 2teaspoon, channa dal 1/2 teaspoon, fenugreek 1 teaspoon, red chilli 10 numbers, haldi powder 1/2 teaspoon, coconut gratings 3 tablespoon,all these ingradients are to be fried dry and ground to a paste.

method:Cut the brinjal into 1 inch blocks. Boil in water and add all the above except toor dal. the dal has to be cooked separately and finally added to the main portion. Seasoning:fry in oil mustard, toor dal and coconut gratings and add to the main dish. Also add coriander leaves and Kari veppu leaves. This dish will have to be made thick and brinjals should not be fully mashed. This dish can be eaten along with rice and chapathis.

Stuffed Brinjal Curry

Split peas dal - 1 1/2 tsp, urud dal - 1 1/2 tsp, coriander seeds - 1 1/2 tsp, whole red peppers - 10, salt to taste Fry the above in one spoon of oil and grind it into a thick paste.Cut 10 small brinjals diagonally so that the stem portion of the brinjal opens up. Stuff the brinjal with the ground paste. Heat oil in a fry pan and add the brinjals, keeping the stove at low heat.Close the pan with a lid and cook for 10 minutes.See that it is not deep fried. Serve hot.

Maida Bonda

Maida or All-purpose-flour -2cups, Rice flour - Half cup, Finely chopped onions - 2 onions, Chillies - 2 nos, Cumin seeds - 1 spoon, Sour curd - 1 cup

Method: Mix all the above ingredients and soak for about one hour.Then take some oil in a pan, put small portions of it in oil,fry them intil they are golden brown.This is good for appetizer.

Rava Bonda

Rava - 3 Cups, Rice Flour - 1 Cup, Curd : 1 Cup, Cashew Bits, Green Chilly 3pcs,Salt to suit taste, Oil for frying.
Mix roasted Rava, Rice flour, Curd, salt , Cashews and Green Chillies to get a semi solid batter. Take small balls and deep fry it in Oil. If needed, coconut shreddings can be added to the batter. Remove from the frying pan after the balls become golden in colour. Serve it with Coconut Chutney. Recipe from Vanitha Thyagu.

Palak Paneer

Boil palak with 3 green chillies , 1/2 onion , salt , 1/2 tsp ginger garlic paste , 1/2 tsp turmeric . cool and grind it . Now take a pan add oil then addsome cumin seeds , mustard seeds , 2 dry red chillies . allow to splutter add in palak paste , 1 glass of milk and mix well. IN a seperate pan add 2 tsp of oil and fry paneer pieces till golden brown in colour . Drain on a paper towel and add to the palak mixture .boil for a few min and serve with hot parathas or puris

Recipe from SATYA

Coconut Milk Pulav

Masala : Ginger - 1" piece, Garlic gloves - 6 to 8, green chillies - 14 to 15. Cut th above into small pieces and grind finely. Ingredients: Coconut Milk (15 oz. Can) - 1, Basmati Rice - 2 cups, Carrots medium sized - 2, Beans - 10 to 15, Grean Peas - 1/4 cup, Cinnamon sticks - 1 or 2, Cloves - 2, Coriander leaves - 7 to 8 stems, salt to taste, veg. Oil or butter - 10 tea spoons. Clean and Soak the rice in hot water for 10 to 15 mints.First put the cooking oil. when oil heats add the cinnamon sticks and cloves. Add the Vegetables (except peas) and fry for some time. Then add the masala paste, salt and fry for some more time. Also add green peas and Coriander leaves and fry. Now pour the Coconut milk and add water for the rest. (Rice and Water should be in 1 : 11/2 proportion). Let this mixture boil nicely. Finally add the rice and cover it. Make the flame low and keep for 20 mints. Open it and mix the cooked pulav gently. Garnish with few fresh coriander leaves

Tomato pickle

Cut the tomatoes into large pieces.Add red chilli powder,a small piece of tamarind and salt.Grind it in a blender to make it into a thick juice.Pout 5 teaspoons of oil in a frypan.Add mustard seeds,fenugreek seeds, and asafoetida(perungayam).When the mustard splatters,add the tomato mixture and fry at low heat with constant frying until it becomes a thick paste.This will taste great with curd rice.

Lime pickle

Fresh lime(large size, thin skin, ripe) - 6
Cut into medium pieces.(Preseve the juice while cutting).Add salt- 4 spoons,red chilli powder - 4 spoons, asafoetida - 1/2 spoon and mix well.
Next day add 1/4 cup of sesame oil and leave it aside.
Next day, add mustard seeds to 4 spoons of oil and when it splatters add fenugreek seeds and asafoetida.Add this to the poickle and mix.Store in refrigerator.

Ginger Pickle

Grate ginger finely.Take oil and add mustard seeds.When it splatters, add fenugreek seed powder an asafoetida.Add grated ginger and fry well till the moisture is gone and it becomes a non-sticky paste.

Tamarind pickle (Pulikkachal)

coriander seeds (Dhaniya), fenugreek seeds, sesame seeds - each 1 spoon asafoetida - 1/4 spoon
Slightly roast the above without oil and grind into fine powder. Pour 3 spoons of oil in a fry pan and add some gram dal and whole red peppers and fry slightly.
Add tamarind juice to this and bring it to boil. Add salt and heat with constant stirring until the mixture becomes thick. Now add the ground powder and stir constantly with heating until it becomes a non-sticky paste. Store in refrigerator.

268. Maavadu (Tender mango pickle)
Grind mustard seeds, crystalline salt, whole red peppers and turmeric poweder- a pinch into a thick paste. Wash the tender mangoes and spread the ground paste on it.

Aavakkai (Mango pickle)

sour mango pieces(medium sized)- 5 cups mustard seed powder - 1 cup
red chilli powder - 1 cup salt - 1 cup
turmeric powder- a pinch, fenugreek seed powder - little mix the above ingredients and add 3 cups of sesame oil.

Gonkura Thokku

Wash the gonkura leaves and dry them on a sheet of paper. Cut into fine pieces.To 5 spoons of oil, add mustard seeds, fenugreek seeds, asafoetida, and add 1 cup of chopped leaves. Fry with constant stirring.Add 1 tsp salt, 2 tsp red chillie powder and cook until it becomes a non-sticky paste.

Curd Vadai

Grind some grated coconut and green chillies into a thick paste.Add this to thick curd and keep it aside. Rinse the required amount of urud dal(black gram) for about 1 1/2 hours.Grind into a thick paste. Add salt, coconut pieces, black whole peppers, and asafoetida.Take a small piece of plantain leaf or plastic sheet of
paper and tap the flour on the sheet into a round flat shape Make a small hole in the middle so that it gets fried uniformly.Drop this carefuly into boiling oil and fry till it turns golden brown.

Cabbage Vadai

Soak 1 cup of urul dal for 1 hour and grind into a thick fine paste.
To 1 volume of this add I volume of finely cut cabbage pieces ,add salt - 3/4 spoon and mix well

Take a plastic sheet of paper and put even sized balls of this and flatten it. Deep fry this in boining oil. Turn over until golden brown in colour and it is fully cooked...

Urud Vadai (Medhu vadai)

Soak 1 cup urud dal in sufficient amt of water for 1 hour and grind into a thick fine flour. Add 1 tsp salt, 2-3 chopped green chillies, 1 tsp whole black peppers, a bunch of curry leaves and mix well. On a plastic piece of paper place a ball of this and flatten it by hand. Deep fry this in oil and turn over until the vada turns golden brown.

Mutton Rogan Josh

An Indian delight made with mutton, can be enjoyed with rice or naan.

Preparation time: 10 minutes
Total time: 1 hour 55 minutes

Yield: 8 servings

Ingredients

2 pounds mutton, cut into small pieces
2 medium onion, chopped
2 medium tomatoes, chopped
1 tablespoon ginger paste
1 tablespoon garlic paste
1/2 tablespoon red chili powder
1 teaspoon kosher salt
1/2 teaspoon turmeric powder
1 bunch of fresh coriander
2 whole green chilies
1/4 cup olive oil
1 cup yogurt
1/2 teaspoon cumin seeds, ground
1/2 teaspoon fennel seeds, ground
1/2 teaspoon of cumin seeds
3 green cardamom pods
4 cups of water
2 tablespoons thinly sliced ginger root, to serve
fresh coriander leaves, for garnish

Method

1. In a large saucepan, combine mutton, water and salt, cover with lid and cook for 1 and ½ hour on low heat or until mutton is tender. Stir occasionally.
2. Heat oil in another large pan or skillet, add cardamom pods and cumin seeds; let them to pop.
3. Add onion and stir-fry until translucent. Then, add ginger paste, garlic paste, tomatoes, red chilies, and turmeric; cook for 5 minutes.
4. Add the cooked mutton and green chilies, stir-fry for 5 minutes.
5. Stir in yogurt; cover with lid and let cook on low flame for 10 minutes or until water has reduced.
6. When the sauce has thickened turn off heat. Sprinkle ground cumin seeds, coriander seed, and fennel seeds. Mix well.
7. Transfer into serving dish, top with ginger slices and chopped fresh coriander leaves.
8. Enjoy.

Nutritional Information:

Energy - 348 calories

Fat - 18.0 g

Carbohydrates - 10.6 g

Protein - 35.2 g

Sodium - 412 mg

Indian Aloo Gobi

This flavourful dish is made with cauliflower, potatoes and Indian spices.

Preparation time: 10 minutes
Total Time: 40 minutes
Yield: 6 servings

Ingredients
1 large cauliflower, cut into small pieces
3 potatoes, peel and cut into cubes
1 onion, thinly sliced
1 teaspoon ginger paste
1/2 teaspoon salt
1 teaspoon garlic paste
1/2 teaspoon turmeric powder
1/2 teaspoon red chili powder
1/4 cup cooking oil
4 tablespoons of tomato paste

1/2 teaspoon cumin seeds
1 bunch of fresh coriander, chopped
2 green chilies, chopped
1/2 teaspoon cumin powder
1/2 teaspoon cinnamon powder
1 cup of water
1 medium tomato, sliced for garnish

Method
1. Heat oil in a saucepan add cumin seeds and let them pop.
2. Add onion slices and cook for 2-3 minutes or until onion becomes translucent. Then, add the tomato paste, garlic paste, ginger paste, red chilli powder, turmeric powder, and salt. Mix thoroughly.
3. Add cauliflower and potatoes, cook for 5 minutes.
4. Add 1 cup of water; cover saucepan with lid and cook for 10 minutes on low flame.
5. Turn off heat when potatoes and cauliflower become tender.
6. Sprinkle cumin powder, cinnamon powder and mix.
7. Garnish with chopped green chillies, coriander and tomatoes.
8. Serve with boiled rice or bread.

Nutritional Information:
Energy - 213 calories
Fat - 9.6 g
Carbohydrates - 29.6 g

Protein - 5.6 g
Sodium - 260 mg

Paratha with Minced Meat

This satisfying recipe will surely become everyone's favourite!

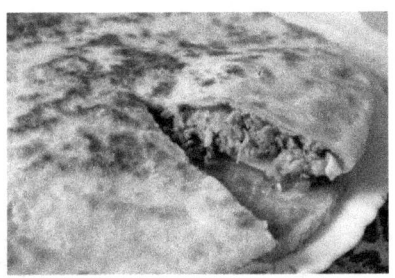

Preparation time: 40 minutes
Total Time: 1 hour 10 minutes
Yield: 8 servings

Ingredients
2 cups mutton, minced
1 onion, finely chopped
1 teaspoon garlic paste
1/2 teaspoon salt
1/2 teaspoon turmeric powder
1/2 teaspoon red chili powder
3 tablespoons of olive oil
2 tablespoons of tomato paste
1 bunch of coriander, chopped

2 green chilies, chopped

1 teaspoon cumin powder

1 teaspoon cinnamon powder

For Dough:

2 cups of wheat flour

1/2 teaspoon salt

1 cup water

4 tablespoons of butter

Method
1. Sift flour and ½ teaspoon of salt, knead a soft dough with water.
2. Cover dough and place aside for 10 minutes.
3. Heat oil in a saucepan add onion and cook for 5 minutes.
4. Add tomato paste, garlic paste, red chili powder, turmeric powder, and salt. Mix well.
5. Add the mutton and stir-fry for 10 minutes or until cooked through.
6. Sprinkle cumin powder, cinnamon powder, chopped green chilies, and coriander. Mix until combined well. Turn off heat.
7. Divide dough in 8 equal parts and roll into even balls.
8. On a clean surface flatten each ball with rolling pin and shape in the form of round bread.
9. Take 1 bread and spread about 3 tablespoons of stuffing, top with another bread and roll out with rolling pin. Press to seal the edges.
10. In a frying pan place 1 tablespoon of butter and put paratha in pan.

11. Flip after 1 minute, place butter on top and flip again.
12. Cook both sides until lightly golden.
13. Serve hot.

Nutritional Information:
Energy - 347 calories
Fat - 16.9 g
Carbohydrates - 27.6 g
Protein - 20.5 g
Sodium - 312 mg

Traditional Palak Paneer

This traditional Indian recipe is made with smooth spinach curry with cottage cheese cubes.

Preparation time: 20 minutes
Total Time: 50 minutes
Yield: 6 servings

Ingredients

2 pounds baby spinach

8 oz. cottage cheese, cubes

1 medium onion, finely chopped

1 teaspoon garlic paste

1/2 teaspoon salt

1/2 teaspoon turmeric powder

1/2 teaspoon red chili powder

1/4 cup olive oil

2 medium tomatoes, chopped

2 green chilies, chopped

1/2 teaspoon cumin powder

1/2 teaspoon cinnamon powder

3 1/2 cups water, divided

Method
1. In a large saucepan boil 3 cups of water on medium heat, add spinach and leave to cook for 3 minutes.
2. Rinse spinach leaves under tap water. Drain.
3. Add spinach into blender and pulse for 1 minutes or until smooth puree is formed.
4. Heat oil in a saucepan add cumin seeds and let it pop.
5. Add onion and stir-fry for 5 minutes.
6. When onion become golden brown add tomatoes, garlic paste, red chili powder, turmeric powder, salt and cook for 5 minutes.
7. Add spinach puree and cook for 10 minutes or until oil leaves the sides of pan.

8. 8. Now add ½ cup of water, chopped green chilies, cover the saucepan with lid and let to cook on slow flame for 5 minutes.
9. Meanwhile fry cheese cubes into frying pan until lightly golden and place aside.
10. Add cheese cubes in spinach puree and combine gently.
11. Turn off heat when spinach curry is smooth, sprinkle cumin powder, cinnamon powder. Mix well.
12. Serve and enjoy.

Nutritional Information:

Energy - 234 calories

Fat - 15.6 g

Carbohydrates - 13.9 g

Protein - 12.5 g

Sodium - 421 mg

Chole Bhature

Spicy, tasty and tempting! This curried dish is made with white chickpeas and served with fried puffed bread.

Preparation time: 40 minutes
Total Time: 1 hour 20 minutes
Yield: 6 servings

Ingredients
2 cups chickpeas, boiled
1 large onion, finely chopped
1 teaspoon garlic paste
1 teaspoon ginger paste
1/2 teaspoon salt
1/2 teaspoon turmeric powder
1/2 teaspoon red chilli powder

2 tablespoons olive oil

1/4 teaspoon cumin powder

1/2 teaspoon cinnamon powder

1/2 teaspoon cumin seeds

1 bay leaf

2 cups water

green chilies and fresh coriander leaves, for garnishing

For Bhature

2 cups wheat flour

1/2 cup semolina

1/2 teaspoon salt

2 tablespoons butter

oil for frying

water for kneading

Method

1. Sift flour and ½ teaspoon of salt, add semolina and knead a soft dough with water.
2. Cover dough and place in freezer for 30 minutes.
3. Heat oil in a saucepan add cumin seeds, bay leaf, and cook until aromatic.
4. Add chopped onion and cook for 5 minutes.
5. Then, add garlic paste, ginger paste, red chilli powder, turmeric powder, salt and mix thoroughly.
6. Add chickpeas and fry for 15 minutes.
7. Now, add the water and cover the saucepan with lid and let to cook on slow flame for 15-20 minutes.

8. Turn off heat when chickpea curry is thickened, sprinkle cumin powder, cinnamon powder and mix.

9. Knead the dough again and form 8 even balls.

10. Roll out each ball in the form of round bread.

11. Heat oil in pan and deep fry bhaturas, press a little with spoon while frying so that bhaturas will puff well.

12. Garnish with green chilies on top, serve and enjoy.

Nutritional Information:
Energy - 375 calories
Fat - 17.6 g
Carbohydrates - 46.5 g
Protein - 8.9 g
Sodium - 175 mg

Curried Spicy Egg

This aromatic spiced sauce is made with onion, tomato, flavoured with basil and topped with boiled eggs.

Preparation time: 15 minutes
Total Time: 35 minutes
   Yield: 4 servings

Ingredients

2 medium onions, finely chopped
4 large eggs, hard boiled, halved
1 cup tomato puree
1 teaspoon garlic paste
2 tablespoon coconut powder
1/2 teaspoon salt
1/2 teaspoon turmeric powder
1/2 teaspoon red chili powder
1/4 teaspoon black pepper
1/4 cup olive oil

1 teaspoon cumin powder
1 teaspoon cinnamon powder
1/2 teaspoon cumin seeds
1 cinnamon stick
2 tablespoon lemon juice
3-4 basil leaves
mint leaves for garnishing

Method
1. Heat oil in a saucepan add cumin seeds, basil leaves, cinnamon stick and let to fry.
2. Add onion, stir-fry until translucent.
3. Then, add tomato puree, garlic paste, coconut powder, ginger paste, black pepper, red chili powder, turmeric powder, and salt. Mix well.
4. Add ½ cup of water and allow to cook for 4 minutes.
5. Stir in cumin powder and cinnamon powder.
6. When the gravy becomes thickened, add the boiled eggs and turn off heat.
7. Drizzle with lemon juice.
8. **Garnish with mint leaves and serve.**

Nutritional Information:
Energy - 241 calories
Fat - 18.9 g
Carbohydrates - 13.7 g
Protein - 7.0 g

Sodium - 367 mg

Chaat Papdi

This thin and crispy crackers are very easy to make!

Preparation time: 20 minutes
Total Time: 35 minutes
   Yield: 8 servings

   Ingredients
1 cup plain flour

1 cup semolina

1/2 teaspoon salt

1 cup of water for kneading

oil for frying

   Method
1. Sift flour and semolina, add salt and knead with water.

2. Dough must be smooth and soft.

3. Cover dough and leave it for 15 minutes.

4. Dust the clean surface with a bit of flour and roll out dough into a thin sheet.

5. Cut it onto small circles using a pastry cutter.

6. Prick with fork so Papdi will not puff.

7. Heat oil in pan and fry Papdi till lightly golden. Drain excess oil using paper towels.

8. Serve and enjoy.

Nutritional Information:

Energy - 212 calories

Fat - 9.5 g

Carbohydrates - 27.1 g

Protein - 4.3 g

Sodium - 148 mg

Pav Bhaji Masala

Traditional recipe made with tomatoes, butter and mashed

potatoes is a sure delight!

Preparation time: 10 minutes
Total Time: 30 minutes
    Yield: 8 servings

Ingredients

1 medium onion, finely chopped
3 potatoes, boiled, mashed
1/4 cup cauliflower, grated
1 cup tomato puree
1 teaspoon garlic paste
1 teaspoon ginger paste
1/2 teaspoon salt
2 tomatoes, chopped

1/2 teaspoon red chili powder

4 tablespoons cooking oil

3 tablespoon lemon juice

2 green chilies, chopped

8 bread buns

4 tablespoons butter

coriander leaves for garnishing

1 lemon, sliced for garnishing

Method
1. Heat oil in a pan and stir-fry onion for 2-3 minutes.
2. Add tomatoes, garlic paste, ginger paste, red chili powder, green chilies, and salt. Stir well.
3. Add tomato puree, cauliflower, mashed potatoes, ¼ cup of water, allow to cook for 2 minutes.
4. Add 2 tablespoons of butter and cover pan with lid, cook on low heat for 5 minutes.
5. Turn off heat when the sauce becomes thick.
6. Drizzle lemon juice.
7. Make a cut from centre of each bun.
8. Heat 1 teaspoon of butter in a pan, place 1 bun and toast from each side.
9. Repeat same process for each bun.
10. Serve with gravy and pavs (buns). Garnish with coriander leaves and lemon slices.

Nutritional Information:

Energy - 303 calories
Fat - 14.3 g
Carbohydrates - 37.6 g
Protein - 8.3 g
Sodium - 407 mg

Traditional Lamb Vindaloo

This traditional Indian recipe is absolutely spicy!

Preparation time: 2 hours
  Total Time: 2 hours 40 minutes
  Yield: 12 servings

   Ingredients
4 pounds boneless lamb, cut into small pieces
1 medium onion, finely chopped
6 garlic cloves, chopped
1 large ginger
1 teaspoon salt
2 whole red chillies
1/2 teaspoon turmeric powder
3 tablespoons cooking oil
2 green cardamoms
3 cloves
1 teaspoon mustard seeds

1 teaspoon cumin seeds
1/4 cup vinegar
3 tablespoons papaya paste
2 cups of water
fresh coriander leaves and ginger for garnishing

Method
1. In a blender add whole red chillies, vinegar, garlic, ginger, cumin seeds, mustard seeds, turmeric powder, and cardamom. Process until smooth.
2. Season lamb with salt, then add the prepared spice mix, papaya paste and marinate it for at least an hour.
3. Heat oil in a saucepan add lamb with its juice, add onion and stir.
4. Fry on medium heat for 10 minutes.
5. Add water and cover with lid cook on low heat for 1 hour or until lamb is tender.
6. **Garnish with coriander leaves and some ginger slices.**

Nutritional Information:
Energy - 293 calories
Fat - 13.4 g
Carbohydrates - 3.3 g
Protein - 37.7 g
Sodium - 298 mg

Traditional Mataba

This fried pastry filled with spicy vegetable is the best treat for everyone!

Preparation time: 30 minutes
Total Time: 50 minutes
 Yield: 8 servings

 Ingredients
1 medium onion, finely chopped
1 cup cauliflower, chopped
2 medium boiled potatoes, mashed
2 cups cabbage, chopped
1 teaspoon garlic paste
1/4 teaspoon salt
2 green chilies, chopped
1/2 teaspoon turmeric powder

1/2 teaspoon cumin powder
2 tablespoons lemon juice
1/4 cup + 2 tablespoons olive oil, divided
2 large eggs

   For dough
2 cups flour
1/2 teaspoon salt
1/2 water

   For dipping sauce
1 cup vinegar
1/2 teaspoon salt
1 tablespoon red chili flakes

Method
1. Sift flour and salt, knead with water to soften dough.
2. Cover dough and let sit for 10 minutes.
3. Heat oil in a saucepan add onion stir for 1 minute.
4. Add garlic paste, red chilli powder, turmeric powder, and salt. Mix thoroughly.
5. Add cabbage, cauliflower, cinnamon powder, cumin powder, lemon juice, green chillies and fry for 2 minutes.
6. Beat egg in bowl and place aside.
7. Divide dough in 8 equal parts and roll into even balls.
8. On a clean surface flatten each ball with rolling pin and shape in the form of round bread.

9. Spread 2 tablespoons of filling, pour 2 tablespoons of egg on filling and shape the round bread in square form.

10. In a frying pan place 1 tablespoon oil and place mataba in pan.

11. Cook from both sides until lightly golden.

12. For sauce mix vinegar, salt and chilli flakes.

13. **Serve hot with chilli sauce.**

Nutritional Information:

Energy - 272 calories

Fat - 10.8 g

Carbohydrates - 36.3 g

Protein - 6.4 g

Sodium - 322 mg

♦♦♦♦♦♦♦♦♦

Curry Malai Kofta

Soft cheesy koftas with rich and creamy gravy.

Preparation time: 35 minutes
Total Time: 60 minutes
    Yield: 6-8 servings

Ingredients

1 cup cottage cheese, crumbled

4 medium potatoes, boiled, mashed

1 cup tomato puree

1/4 cup coconut powder

1 onion, chopped

1 teaspoon garlic paste

1 tablespoon cornstarch

1/2 teaspoon salt

1 cup heavy cream

1/2 teaspoon red chilli powder

2 green chilies, chopped
1/2 teaspoon turmeric powder
1/2 teaspoon dry coriander powder
1/2 teaspoon cumin powder
1/2 teaspoon cinnamon powder
1 bunch of coriander, chopped
cooking oil, for deep frying

Method
1. In a large bowl add cottage cheese, mashed potatoes, ½ teaspoon salt, green chilies, chopped coriander, and cornstarch. Mix well and make small round balls.
2. Heat oil in pan deep fry cheese balls till golden. Drain excess oil using paper towels and set aside.
3. Heat 1 tablespoon oil in a saucepan add onion stir for 1 minute.
4. Add garlic paste, red chilli powder, turmeric powder, and salt.
5. Add tomato puree, coconut powder and stir.
6. Add cream and mix, sprinkle cumin powder, coriander powder, cinnamon powder and toss. Turn off heat.
7. Place cheese koftas in a serving dish. Pour gravy on top and garnish with coriander leaves.
8. **Serve hot.**

Nutritional Information:

Energy - 374 calories
Fat - 23.7 g
Carbohydrates - 32.3 g
Protein - 9.8 g
Sodium - 384 mg

♦♦♦♦♦♦♦♦♦

Kakori Kebab

These delightful kebabs are great option for a dinner party.

Preparation time: 15 minutes
Total Time: 30 minutes
   Yield: 6 servings

Ingredients
2 cups meat, minced
1 onion, chopped
1 teaspoon garlic paste
1 teaspoon salt
1/2 teaspoon red chili powder
2 green chilies, chopped
1 teaspoon coriander seeds, ground
1/2 teaspoon cumin powder
1/2 teaspoon cinnamon powder

1 bunch of coriander, chopped
3 bread slices, shredded
oil for frying

Method
1. In a large bowl add meat, salt, green chilies, bread slices, red chilies, coriander powder, garlic paste, chopped coriander, cinnamon powder, and cumin powder. Knead with clean hand until combined well.
2. Shape meat around skewers and place in a platter.
3. Heat 2 tablespoon oil in pan shallow fry kebabs till golden brown.
4. **Serve and enjoy.**

Nutritional Information:
Energy - 257 calories
Fat - 18.8 g
Carbohydrates - 7.7 g
Protein - 14.1 g
Sodium - 581 mg

♦♦♦♦♦♦♦♦♦

Cucumber Raita with Dill

This Indian recipe is a combination of cucumber, yogurt, fresh

mint and dill.

Preparation time: 10 minutes
Total Time: 15 minutes
    Yield: 4 servings

Ingredients
1 cup plain yogurt
1 medium onion, chopped
2 medium cucumbers, chopped
2 tablespoon lemon juice
1 garlic clove, minced
1/2 teaspoon salt

1 green chilli, chopped
1/2 teaspoon black pepper
1/2 teaspoon coriander seeds, ground
1/2 teaspoon cumin seeds, ground
1 bunch of mint leaves
1/2 cup dill weed, chopped

Method
1. In a large bowl, mix all the ingredients well. Transfer to a serving dish. Garnish with some chopped cucumbers and dill.
2. Serve and enjoy.

Nutritional Information:
- Energy - 53 calories
- Fat - 0.7 g
- Carbohydrates - 9.0 g
- Protein - 3.4 g
- Sodium - 181 mg

Indian Rajma

This super delicious recipe will definitely make you feel delighted.

Preparation time: 10 minutes
Total Time: 45 minutes
    Yield: 8 servings

Ingredients
1 cup red beans, boiled
1 onion, chopped
3 tomatoes, chopped
6 garlic cloves, minced
1/2 teaspoon salt
1/2 red chili flakes
1/2 teaspoon turmeric powder
2 green chilies

1/2 teaspoon coriander, ground

1/2 teaspoon cumin seeds

1/2 cinnamon powder

1 bunch of fresh coriander, chopped

1/4 cup olive oil

1 cup of water

Method

1. Heat oil in a pan, cumin seeds, onion and stir-fry until translucent.

2. Add tomatoes, garlic, red chilli flakes, turmeric powder, ground coriander, and salt. Cook, stirring for 5 minutes.

3. Add boiled beans, green chilies and water; cover with lid cook on low flame for 20 minutes.

4. Turn off heat when the gravy become thick.

5. Sprinkle cinnamon powder and stir.

6. **Garnish with coriander leaves and serve.**

Nutritional Information:

Energy - 158 calories

Fat - 7.2 g

Carbohydrates - 18.6 g

Protein - 6.0 g

Sodium - 155 mg

Aloo Mutter

This is a wonderful, easy and healthy dish made with potato,

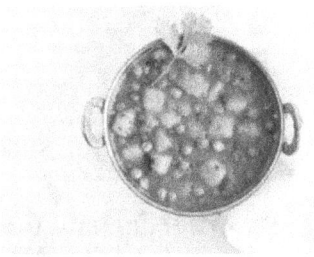

peas, and curry.

Preparation time: 10 minutes
Total Time: 40 minutes
Yield: 6 servings

Ingredients

1 cup frozen green peas, thawed
3 potatoes, peel and cut into cubes
1 onion, thinly sliced
1 teaspoon ginger paste
1/2 teaspoon salt
1 teaspoon garlic paste
1/2 teaspoon turmeric powder
1/2 teaspoon red chilli powder

2 tablespoons cooking oil

2 tomatoes, chopped

1 bunch of cilantro, chopped

2 green chillies, chopped

1/2 teaspoon cumin powder

1/2 teaspoon cinnamon powder

1 cup of water

Method
1. Heat oil in a saucepan and add onion slices and cook for 2 minutes.
2. When onion become translucent, add the tomatoes, garlic paste, ginger paste, red chilli powder, turmeric powder, and salt. Mix thoroughly.
3. **Add peas and potatoes and to cook for 10 minutes.**
4. **Then, add 1 cup of water, cover saucepan with lid and cook for 20 minutes on low flame.**
5. When potatoes and peas become soft, turn off heat.
6. Sprinkle cumin powder and cinnamon powder. Mix well. Garnish with chopped green chilies, cilantro, and tomatoes.
7. Serve and enjoy.

Nutritional Information:

Energy - 228 calories

Fat - 7.4 g

Carbohydrates - 36.6 g

Protein - 5.7 g

Sodium - 310 mg

Indian Aloo Palak

This Indian dish is made with spinach and potatoes.

Preparation time: 20 minutes
Total Time: 45 minutes
 Yield: 4 servings

 Ingredients

1 lb. fresh spinach, coarsely chopped

3 potatoes, peeled and cut into cubes

1 large onion, thinly sliced

2 medium tomatoes

1 teaspoon garlic paste

1/2 teaspoon turmeric powder

1/2 teaspoon red chili powder

1/2 teaspoon salt

2 tablespoons cooking oil

2 tomatoes, chopped

2 green chillies, chopped

1/2 teaspoon cumin powder

1/2 teaspoon cinnamon powder

2 cups of water

Method
1. Heat oil in a saucepan and add onion slices and cook for 2 minutes.
2. When the onion becomes translucent, add tomatoes, garlic paste, red chili powder, turmeric powder, and salt. Mix well.
3. **Then, add potatoes and cook for 5 minutes.**
4. **Add 2 cups of water, green chilies, cover saucepan with lid and cook for 20 minutes on low flame. Add the spinach and cook further 3-5 minutes.**
5. Sprinkle cumin powder and cinnamon powder.
6. Transfer to a serving dish and serve.

Nutritional Information:

Energy - 179 calories

Fat - 7.5 g

Carbohydrates - 25.6 g

Protein - 4.9 g

Sodium - 361 mg

Bhindi Masala Fry

This easy to make okra recipe will definitely become everyone's favourite.

Preparation time: 25 minutes
Total Time: 50 minutes
    Yield: 6 servings

Ingredients

1 lb. okra
1 medium onion, thinly sliced
1/2 teaspoon salt
1 teaspoon garlic paste
1/2 teaspoon turmeric powder
1/2 teaspoon red chili powder
1/4 cup olive oil
3 medium tomatoes, chopped
2 green chilies, chopped
1/2 teaspoon cumin powder

1/2 teaspoon cinnamon powder

1/2 teaspoon coriander seed, ground

1/2 teaspoon aniseeds, ground

lemon slices, to serve

Method
1. Wash okra, let to dry, remove base and stalk and make a cut from centre or each okra.
2. Heat oil in a saucepan and add onion slices and cook for 1 minute.
3. **Add tomatoes, garlic paste, red chilli powder, green chilies, turmeric powder, and salt. Cook, stirring for 5 minutes.**
4. **Then, add okra and cook for 5-7 minutes.**
5. Sprinkle cumin powder, cinnamon, coriander, ground aniseeds and mix thoroughly. Remove from heat.
6. Garnish with lemon slices and serve with chapatti/bread.

Nutritional Information:

Energy - 200 calories

Fat - 14.3 g

Carbohydrates - 16.0 g

Protein - 3.6 g

Sodium - 308 mg

Chana Pulao

Chana pulao is spicy, aromatic and delicious dish by all means, made with chickpeas and rice.

Preparation time: 35 minutes
Total Time: 60 minutes
    Yield: 6 servings

Ingredients

1 cup rice, uncooked
2 tablespoons cooking oil
1 black cardamom
1 teaspoon cumin seeds, ground
3 cloves
3 green cardamoms
2 medium onions, thinly sliced
2 cups chickpeas, boiled

2 medium tomatoes, chopped

2 green chilies, chopped

1/2 teaspoon cumin powder

1/2 teaspoon cinnamon powder

1/2 teaspoon salt

1 tablespoon garlic paste

1/4 teaspoon turmeric powder

1/2 teaspoon chili powder

2 cups of water

Method
1. Wash rice and soak in water for 30 minutes.
2. Meanwhile, heat oil in a saucepan, add the black cardamom, cumin seeds, cloves, green cardamom, and stir for 30 seconds.
3. **Then, add onion and stir-fry until translucent.**
4. **Add chickpeas, garlic paste, cinnamon powder, cumin powder, red chilli powder, turmeric powder, salt and fry for 10 minutes.**
5. Add tomatoes, green chillies and cook for 5 minutes.
6. Stir in 2 cups of water, cover with lid and let cook for 10 minutes on high heat.
7. **Add soaked rice and cook on high heat till bubbles come on the surface of rice.**
8. Cover pan with lid, cook for 20 minutes on low heat.
9. Transfer into serving dish and serve.

Nutritional Information:
Energy - 266 calories
Fat - 6.4 g
Carbohydrates - 44.8 g
Protein - 7.8 g
Sodium - 206 mg

Banana Chips

This crisp, crunchy, and spicy banana chip recipe is great option for snack.

Preparation time: 5 minutes
Total Time: 10 minutes
   Yield: 8 servings

Ingredients
6 raw plantain bananas
1/2 teaspoon salt
1/2 teaspoon garlic powder
1/2 teaspoon red chilli powder
1/2 teaspoon black pepper
1 cup cooking oil

Method
1. Heat oil in a large pan.
2. Meanwhile, thinly peel bananas and slice thinly. Place them in the pan with hot oil.
3. **Fry on high flame for 3-5 minutes.**
4. **Stir and when banana chips are crisp, transfer into a serving platter.**
5. Sprinkle salt, chilli powder, black pepper, and garlic powder. Toss to combine well.
6. Enjoy.

Nutritional Information:
Energy - 287 calories

Fat - 14.0 g

Carbohydrates - 43.2 g

Protein - 1.6 g

Sodium - 296 mg

♦♦♦♦♦♦♦♦♦

Baingan Barta

This flavourful dish is made with brinjal and can be served as a main course.

Preparation time: 15 minutes
Total Time: 40 minutes
      Yield: 4 servings

Ingredients
3 large brinjal (eggplant)
1 large onion, thinly sliced
2 tomatoes, chopped
1/2 teaspoon salt
1 teaspoon garlic paste
1/2 teaspoon turmeric powder
1/2 teaspoon red chilli powder
1/4 cup cooking oil

2 green chilies, chopped

1/2 teaspoon dry coriander powder

2 green chilies, chopped

Method
1. Wash brinjals and place directly on high flame for 1 minute till skin of brinjal become golden brown. Repeat same process for all brinjal.
2. Roughly chop brinjal and place aside.
3. **Heat oil in a saucepan and add onion slices and cook for 2 minutes.**
4. **When onion become translucent add tomatoes, garlic paste, red chilli powder, turmeric powder, salt and fry for 10 minutes.**
5. Now add brinjals and cook for 15 minutes.
6. Add green chillies, dry coriander powder, toss well and turn off heat.
7. Serve with chapatti/bread.

Nutritional Information:

Energy - 248 calories

Fat - 14.6 g

Carbohydrates - 29.7 g

Protein - 5 g

Sodium - 307 mg

Dum Aloo

This simple and spicy dish is made with potatoes and tomato gravy.

Preparation time: 10 minutes
Total Time: 35 minutes
   Yield: 4 servings

Ingredients
4 large potatoes
1/4 cup cooking oil
1/2 teaspoon cumin seeds
1 large onion, thinly sliced
2 medium tomatoes, chopped
1/2 teaspoon salt
1 teaspoon garlic paste
1/2 teaspoon turmeric powder
1/2 teaspoon red chili powder

1/2 teaspoon coriander seeds, ground

2 green chilies, chopped

3 tablespoon lemon juice

1/2 teaspoon cinnamon powder

1/2 cup water

Method
1. Heat 2 cups of water. Add potatoes and boil till soft.
2. Heat oil in a saucepan and add cumin seed, stir-fry for 1 minute.
3. **Then, add onion slices and stir until translucent. Add the tomatoes, garlic paste, red chilli powder, turmeric powder, and salt; cook, stirring for 10 minutes.**
4. **Peel boiled potatoes, cut into large cubes and add into tomato mixture, cook for 5 minutes.**
5. Add ½ cup water, green chilies and coriander; cook for 5 minutes on low heat.
6. Turn off heat, sprinkle cinnamon powder, drizzle with lemon juice and mix well.
7. Serve with chapatti/bread.

Nutritional Information:

Energy - 272 calories

Fat - 9.6 g

Carbohydrates - 43.2 g

Protein - 4.9 g

Sodium - 216 mg

Indian Fish Fry

This delicious, soft and crunchy fish recipe is the easiest and fastest way to make everyone happy.

Preparation time: 40 minutes
Total Time: 60 minutes
Yield: 4 servings

Ingredients

4 (5 oz.) fish fillets
2 tablespoons turmeric powder
4 tablespoons wheat flour
1 teaspoon salt
1 tablespoon garlic paste
1 teaspoon chili powder
5 tablespoons chickpea flour

4 tablespoons lemon juice

cooking oil for frying

Method

1. In a large platter place fish fillets, sprinkle turmeric powder, wheat flour and rub with hand to coat well with seasoning. Cover fish and let rest for 20 minutes. After that rinse fish well.
2. Combine salt, red chilli powder, garlic, lemon juice, and chickpea flour in a shallow bowl. Add the fish and rub to coat well. Let sit for 20 minutes.
3. **Heat oil on high flame, then fry fish fillets till golden brown.**
4. **Transfer into a serving platter.**
5. Serve and enjoy.

Nutritional Information:

Energy - 296 calories

Fat - 18.8 g

Carbohydrates - 19.7 g

Protein - 14.1 g

Sodium - 508 mg

Aloo Tiki

This appetizer is so delicious. It is made with boiled potatoes, chickpea flour, and spices.

Preparation time: 30 minutes
Total Time: 50 minutes
    Yield: 8 servings

Ingredients
5 large potatoes, boiled
1 large onion, finely chopped
5 tablespoons chickpea flour
1 teaspoon salt
1 tablespoon chili powder
1 bunch of fresh coriander
2 green chilies, chopped
1/2 teaspoon coriander seeds, ground
1/2 teaspoon cumin powder
1/2 teaspoon cinnamon powder

cooking oil for frying

Method
1. In a bowl add boiled potatoes, chopped onion, fresh coriander, green chilies, red chilies, salt, dry coriander powder, cinnamon powder, cumin powder chickpea flour and mash with potato masher.
2. Make round cutlets with mixture and place into a plate.
3. **Freeze for 15 minutes before frying.**
4. **Now heat 2 tablespoons of oil in a non-stick shallow pan and fry cutlets till lightly golden.**
5. Drain excess oil and transfer into serving platter.
6. Serve and enjoy.

Nutritional Information:
Energy - 241 calories
Fat - 7.4 g
Carbohydrates - 40.2 g
Protein - 4.9 g
Sodium - 317 mg

www.ingramcontent.com/pod-product-compliance
Lightning Source LLC
Chambersburg PA
CBHW071832080526
44589CB00012B/988